CONTENT MARKETING SECRETS

By

Marc Guberti

Copyright Notice

YOUR FREE GIFT

As a way of thanking you for your purchase, I am offering you a free ticket to the Content Marketing Success Summit.

The Content Marketing Success Summit showcases an ever growing list of speakers who will teach you how to create, promote, and optimize your content—and use that content to generate a full-time income.

If you are interested in achieving a full-time income from your content brand, then I recommend getting your free ticket for the **Content Marketing Success Summit** which contains the insights that will allow you to reach the next level.

contentmarketingsuccesssummit.com

TABLE OF CONTENTS

Part 3: Social Media Marketing

Part 4: Content Monetization

INTRODUCTION

The rise of technology has led to new achievements and products and services that now form a central part of our lives. Computers and cell phones were created a few decades ago, and now we can't live without them. With the rise of this technology led to the creation of a new marketing platform that tipped the scales and gave anyone a chance to stand out and do what they love. We now refer to this marketing platform as a content brand, your home on the web where you can craft content—blog posts, videos, podcast episodes, and more—that can be seen by anyone in the world.

When blogs were first created, many people saw them as online diaries. Now, people see blogs as money-generators. Podcasts and videos were adopted later on. Case studies of content creators making thousands and even millions of dollars from their craft led to well established organizations, stay at home moms, employees, and just about everyone else creating their own blogs, channels, and podcasts. People want to reach the gold-mine of the content landscape. At one point, not too long ago, the entire concept of your own blog, channel, and podcast seemed impossible. Now they are a part of every day life.

So now here we stand. Blog posts, videos, podcast episodes, and other forms of content dominate the web and our culture. Top brands craft a variety of types of content, and anyone with a computer and content can strike it rich. The best part is that you get to do it all from the comfort of your home.

However, just like anything else in life, the revenue does not come fast. Some content creators go at it for *years* before making full-time incomes. Other content creators give up in the journey and potentially miss that big increase in traffic and subscribers that could have made the difference between no income and a full-time income. Content brands provide their set of unprecedented opportunities, but it also provides its set of challenges. Any successful content creator who talks about his/her success also has stories of hardships, regrets, and mistakes.

Sure, it takes a while to make money with a content brand, but once you start to generate revenue from your brand, the sky is the limit. You'll be ecstatic when you make your first dollar on the web. One dollar isn't enough to make a full-time income, but it is the beginning of something grand. I will never forget when my books and training courses got their first sales. That first sale is the beginning of something great.

Now comes the popular question that is almost as old as content creation itself: "How do I make an income by creating content? How do I get the same results as the people who now make six, seven, and eight figure incomes from their content brands?"

This book is an answer to that question. After years of analyzing case studies and growing my own content brand into a dominant player within my niche, I decided to create a valuable resource for any blogger, podcaster, YouTuber, or combination of the three regardless of where you are in your journey.

My Content Brand Journey

I will never forget the moment I created my first blog. This was long before I created my YouTube channel and became the host of the Breakthrough Success Podcast. On a hot summer day, my brother and I were bored. We couldn't think of anything to do, and Googling "what to do when you are bored" doesn't work very well. We went to our parents for advice, and they suggested creating blogs. They didn't have blogs of their own, but we took their suggestion to heart. It turns out that during this time, MLBlogs were still intact. MLBlogs were blogs you created with an account on the Major League Baseball website. You could have the background of the blog be your team's logo, and you could write anything you wanted about your team. My brother chose to write about the New York Mets, and I chose to write about the Boston Red Sox.

Growing up as a Boston Red Sox fan in New York is a herculean effort, and now I had a blog about the Boston Red Sox. Some people asked me if I was born in Boston and then moved to New York. What makes the story all the more bizarre is that my father is a dedicated Yankees fan who knows plenty about his team's history. He drives me and the family up to Boston every year so we can watch the Red Sox play some games at Fenway Park.

Here I was with my own blog. I wrote about the players and some of the games. I was getting a feel for blogging, and initially, it was more of a hobby. As an 11-year-old at the time, I did not think of blogging or content brands in general as a way to generate full-time income. I simply saw blogging as a way to pass the time. It was something I did when I felt like it and had nothing else to do. On that summer day, I wrote my first blog post, and now anyone in the world could view my content. I became a part of the ever growing clan of content creators.

Hitting the publish button for the first time can be a bit scary. Once you hit that publish button, there is literally no turning back. Your content is on the web and anyone can view it. Your first blog post is up, and now the next step is to write more blog posts.

I wrote several blog posts for my Red Sox blog, and I got some engagement. Nothing legendary, but enough engagement to give me motivation to continue. Soon enough, blogging emerged as one of my top hobbies. What was initially a last resort after getting bored one summer day now became my number one choice.

Along the journey, I struggled with consistently writing blog posts. Little to my knowledge when I first started, just because you are a big fan of something does not mean it is easy for you to write about that topic. I continued to cheer on the Red Sox, but I preferred to cheer for them than write blog posts about every game. I became an inconsistent blogger, but I still wrote content for that blog. It was all I had, and I knew that stopping now meant throwing it all away.

In 2011, MLBlogs upgraded its service, and in this upgrade, all users were required to join WordPress. This decision by MLBlogs was a pivotal moment for my journey. Joining WordPress opened the door to an easy way to create a blog about any topic I desired. I was no longer limited to baseball related blog posts. I could cheer for my team without having to write a blog post about them the next day (or whenever I got to it).

Remember that if you ever lose joy writing blog posts for a particular blog, you can create a new blog and focus on that new blog at any time.

Since I could now create a blog about almost any topic I desired, I decided to create a blog about Yugioh Cards. I took this blog seriously for a long period of time, and it got over 500 daily visitors at its prime. The blog made a small amount of revenue, but for a long time, I wanted this blog to be the money-maker. I easily updated it every day, and I enjoyed updating it. Now, blogging was at the crossroads of hobby and true passion.

I wanted to bring more traffic to my Yugioh Blog, so I decided to create a Twitter account and do some research to see how my Twitter account would lead to more traffic for my Yugioh Blog. The learning curve was incredible, but once I mastered Twitter and was growing my audience, digital marketing became another passion of mine.

At this point, I made enough money to prove to myself and my family that I could make a full-time income by blogging. I decided to pay for a WordPress.org blog which would be all about digital marketing. For several months, I updated the digital marketing blog and the Yugioh Blog simultaneously. I was writing two blog posts every day. Soon enough, most of my friends stopped playing with Yugioh Cards, and I stopped myself, so digital marketing took over as my top passion.

It took me a few months to finally stop updating the Yugioh Blog. It was getting difficult to continue updating the blog when I wasn't playing the game anymore, but the decision was just as difficult. I stopped updating a blog that was getting over 500 daily visitors to basically start all over again with a blog about digital marketing (the digital marketing blog averaged anywhere from 20-50 daily visitors when I made this shift).

It was a difficult decision, but is was the best decision I could have made in that situation. Focusing on the digital marketing blog allowed me to establish myself as one of the top experts in my niche. In less than two years, I went from having a small social media audience to building up to over a 250,000 targeted social media followers. My digital marketing blog quickly transcended my Yugioh Blog, and digital marketing is something I will stick with for a very long time.

The decision I made allowed me to find my niche. Giving up on a blog I brought from no audience to hundreds of daily visitors was scary. Regardless of how many visitors your blog gets, if you are no longer passionate about your blog's topic, then something must change. Your entire blog must get transformed, or you must create a new blog and abandon the old one, even if that old blog is doing well.

Today, I continue writing digital marketing related blog posts and have created dozens of products ranging from books to training courses. My mission is to empower others so they can take their lives to the next level while spreading the message that age is not a limit to success.

Let's Create Your Story

Just like any other content creator, I started out with no audience. However, I shifted my focus from multiple blogs. I created blogs about the Boston Red Sox, Yugioh Cards, LEGOs, and video games just to name a few of the blogs that started. Now, I have chosen one niche to dominate—digital marketing—and since then, I also have a podcast and YouTube channel.

I want you to have your own success story with your own content brand. I want you to focus on one niche for your content brand and then dominate that niche. I want you to get thousands of visitors every month. I will show you how you can generate an income from your efforts.

Regardless of where you are right now, your story is incomplete. My story is incomplete. There's still a lot more I can do. Your story can still develop. Twists and turns are part of the process. If the transformation hasn't happened yet, there's still plenty of hope. In order to end up with a story you are proud of, you must have these two things:

1. The right knowledge
2. A strong belief in your ability to succeed

Having the right knowledge and implementing the tactics you learn will help towards building the strong belief in your ability to succeed. The deeper you go into your journey, the more you'll believe in yourself. This book is designed to provide you with the knowledge and the seeds that allow you to build a strong belief in your ability to become successful.

Ready to learn what it takes to become a successful content creators? Ready to acquire all of the knowledge you need? Ready to establish a strong belief in your ability to succeed? I'm about to reveal everything… right now.

PART 1:

CONTENT CREATION

Every piece of content you will ever see on the web is nothing more than one idea seen to completion. The passion-fueled ideas made their way to their respective audiences in forms such as blog posts, videos, and podcast episodes.

Some of these forms of content take several hours to craft. Most of your visitors will go through them in a few minutes. By creating a legendary experience for your visitors during those few minutes, they'll come back for more. Content provides a legendary experience when it entertains, empowers, or educates. Some pieces of content leverage two or even three of those criterion, but every successful piece of content is primarily focused on at least one of the three criteria.

While this paints a lovely picture for content creation, there's plenty of work involved. In this part of the book, we will explore some secrets to crafting higher value content in a shorter period of time. The reason we begin with content creation in a content marketing book is because you can't promote the content unless you can consistently create new content. Content creation is the lifeblood of content marketing. Without the content, there's no content marketing.

Chapter 1:

IDENTIFYING & IMPLEMENTING IDEAS

Ideas are the seeds for published content, and with enough nurturing, those seeds grow into mighty trees. Consistently publishing valuable content requires us to continuously cultivate the content ideas that will eventually become published content. The importance of idea generation has resulted three distinct groups of content creators.

Group #1: Content creators who struggle to think of new ideas

Group #2: Content creators with many ideas but a lack of clarity of where to start

Group #3: Content creators with many ideas and total clarity of where to start

Of the groups, Group #1 is the worst and Group #3 is the best. The reason Group #1 is worse than Group #2 is because it's better to struggle over which ideas to tackle first than it is to have no ideas at all.

However, content creators typically shift from group to group. Once a content creator in Group #2 has finally turned all of the ideas into published content, that same person may fall back into Group #1 as the temporarily struggle to think of new ideas begins.

Every content creator wants to be in Group #3. You'll learn how to get there with an unlimited fountain of ideas and clarity of where to start.

Get Inspired By Your Pre-Existing Line Of Content

"Come up with a content idea." It's amazing how this one request can lead to a big blank. This big blank occurs as the mind tries to conjure different content ideas. While conjuring up ideas, the mind is trying to decipher which ideas you haven't covered yet.

For instance, I just thought of writing a blog post containing five tips to grow your Twitter audience. However, I have covered this topic so many times that I am in the need of a new idea. So the challenge isn't coming up with an idea. The challenge is coming up with an entirely new idea from your pre-existing line of content.

Since you are looking for an entirely new idea from your pre-existing line of content, it makes sense that you use your old content as a compass. When I feel stuck, I read through some of my blog posts with these questions:

- What did I miss?
- What could I have elaborated on?
- Which blog post, podcast episode, or video can I turn into a series or a Part Two?
- Can I talk about this same topic in a different way?

Asking these four questions as you go through your older content will open the door to a fountain of new content ideas inspired by your older content.

The Best System For Getting Inspiration From Others

If you don't have much of your own content to go by, seeking inspiration from others will grant you more content ideas. This is also a solid approach for people who have published thousands of blog posts, videos, and podcast episodes.

The next time you find yourself on a blog in your niche, look at the headlines of the blog posts. Some of the blog post headlines you encounter will instantly give you ideas for your own content. For the blog posts you want to read, don't read with learning as the exclusive purpose. Read with the mindset of finding a content idea. Sometimes I re-read other people's individual blog posts just with the mindset of coming up with more ideas.

Use their headlines and their best content as your inspiration as you read through the content. While the blog post themselves can ignite your idea generation efforts, there's one more source of content ideas. It's the most valuable, but also the most forgotten.

At the end of most blog posts is a comments section. You'll see some grateful comments from people who enjoyed the blog post, thus reaffirming the idea that the content was valuable. You'll also see discussions happen where people share additional insights. Those additional insights can inspire content ideas.

The best comments for content idea inspiration are the questions. Questions indicated a topic that needed more coverage to form a more complete blog post. No matter how well you write the blog post, readers will always have questions. If you know the answers, post your answers in the comments section of that blog, even if it isn't your blog. Your posted answer then becomes the outline for your next blog post and give you some extra exposure.

You can take the commenting method further by searching for questions in your niche on Quora. I regularly hunt for questions on Quora and answer them while including a relevant link to one of my pieces of content. Not only do I get more traffic, but I can go back to the questions and my answers. I can then choose the best topics and use my answers to form a blog post outline. Writing detailed answers will help you with crafting your content for a blog post, video, or podcast episode. As of writing, I prefer to turn my answers into blog posts.

Getting Inspiration From Other's Videos and Podcasts

I prefer getting inspiration by reading blog posts and their headlines because it is easier to skim through a blog post than it is to skim through a video or podcast. However, videos and podcasts are both viable forms of content to find inspiration. My initial approach for these two content production mediums would be the same for a blog—skim the headlines.

You won't watch every video or podcast episode, but by skimming the headlines, you'll surround yourself with more content ideas that can inspire some of your own. Once you decide to watch a video or podcast episode, listen to what the person is saying while thinking of the topic as a whole. Write notes based on what you learn AND based on content ideas you think of while engaging with the content. This open-minded approach geared towards idea acquisition will help you come up with more content ideas.

Lately, I've become more attracted to podcast episodes. While I'd prefer a blog post (better yet, a paperback or hardcover book) any day, the listening mechanic creates more possibilities. For instance, I can listen to a podcast while walking the dog. I've never seen someone master the art of walking a dog while reading a book without looking up and down many times. Driving is another activity where you can't read but you can listen to a podcast episode. However, if I'm in the car for the long haul, I prefer an audiobook.

Choosing The Right Content Ideas

Not all content ideas are created equal. Some content ideas are naturally better than others, but here's the important question: What makes one content idea better than another?

A content idea is either worthless or pure gold depending on its context. Some of my spare time goes towards analyzing the stock market. I can write a blog post about stocks, but while it would be valuable in some contexts, it wouldn't be valuable in the context of my content brand.

People don't think about me when they think of the stock market. People think about me when they think of digital marketing, entrepreneurship, and productivity. This is a basic example of avoiding topics that extend beyond your niche. If you write about too many topics, your readers won't know what topic you focus on. If they don't know what topic you focus on, they will neither remember you nor stick around.

But what if you are in the social media marketing space, and you've got to decide between writing a blog post about YouTube or a blog post about Facebook?

Here's my seemingly unrelated but completely related question: When would the blog post get published?

When I hosted the Content Marketing Success Summit, it was *very easy* for me to choose which content ideas I focused on. I exclusively focused on the content marketing pieces. That meant writing blog posts focused on content marketing several weeks before the summit. It meant strategically choosing and interviewing the right podcast guests at the right time. Two months before my virtual summit, I searched for more guests with a focus on content marketing. I even invited some of those guests to speak at the Content Marketing Success Summit.

When I hosted the Productivity Virtual Summit, it was the same story with a different cast. Leading up to the summit, I exclusively focused on publishing new content on productivity. By leveraging this strategy, I warmed my audience up to productivity related articles, episodes, and videos. That warm up perfectly led into the Productivity Virtual Summit. I had conditioned my audience to be ready for the summit.

To answer your question about the YouTube blog post VS the Facebook blog post, it depends on your overall strategy. If you are launching a Facebook ads course in two months, write the blog post about Facebook. Hold off on the YouTube blog post until you're done launching the Facebook ads course. Your focus leading into the course promotion is warming your audience up to desire the benefits that you'll offer in your product.

Putting This On Paper

If you ask me what products I'm creating and promoting within the next year, I can tell you. The Content Marketing Success Summit's promotion started in the beginning of May 2017. The moment that initial promotion began, I had my promotional calendar planned out past March 2018.

By planning out the promotion and creation of products that far out, I could readily and strategically plan out my content ideas as well. I knew what type of content I needed to publish on my blog, YouTube channel, and podcast during this timeframe. By theming each of my cycles based on what I was promoting, it was easier for me to come up with the ideas.

You may be wondering, "Marc, this is great, but how do I actually put this on paper?"

A quick Google search will lead you to victory. You can search for an image of a calendar containing a specific month and the days of the month. You can find calendars for this year, the following year, and many others. You can go very far in the future with this approach. For instance, I know that, as long as I make it to my 100th birthday, it will be celebrated on a Friday. You don't have to plan several decades into the future. To start, you only need to plan at least three months in the future. Get involved with someone else's product launch or create your own product. That way, you can follow a content theme that warms your audience and results in more sales.

Most of the content you create won't result in direct revenue, but content indirectly contributes to your revenue by warming up your visitors to certain products and turning visitors into subscribers (and eventually customers).

Write content ideas on different days of the month you decided to print out. That way, you'll have deadlines for your content ideas under your content theme for a particular cycle. Once you have the content ideas in place, it's time to create the actual content.

Outlining Your Idea With The Socratic Method

The more time you spend outlining your idea, the less time it will take for you to complete that idea. One of my favorite ways to outline an idea is to start by listing all of the possible key points I can cover within the content.

For instance, an article on three ways to get more retweets might look like this. Notice how I don't number them in case I want to cover them in a different order.

3 Ways To Get More Retweets On Twitter

Tweet more frequently

Grow a targeted audience

Tweet more of what your audience wants

With this basic outline, I can easily produce valuable content, but to take your value to the next level, you can use the Socratic Method to expand on your topic. You can anticipate gaps in your content and fill them up. For instance, I can say, "Tweet more frequently and get more retweets," but you might not know how to tweet more frequently without spending several hours on Twitter each day.

I ask myself at least three questions about each key point as if I knew nothing about the topic. Here's what the same outline looks like with the Socratic Method.

3 Ways To Get More Retweets On Twitter

Tweet more frequently

— What tools should I use to tweet more frequently?

— How much is too much? Is there a limit?

— How can I tweet more frequently without spending countless hours on Twitter?

— Why is this even important?

Grow a targeted audience

— How can I tell if I have a targeted audience?

— What are some tools I can use to speed up the process?

— How can I grow my audience without a big time investment?

Tweet more of what your audience wants

— How do I determine what my audience wants?

— What do I tweet before I know what my audience wants?

— What am I supposed to do with this knowledge?

I can rattle off the answers to all of those questions, but the more advanced you are in your niche, the less you think about the beginner and even intermediate who sees some of this as jargon. Don't assume everyone knows the same things as you do.

The Socratic Method creates deeper content and ultimately turns 500-800 word blog posts into the 2,000-3,000 word blog posts (or turns 2 minute videos into 8-10 minute videos) that perform better on search engines. Most importantly, you are producing a more valuable piece of content that adds more value to your audience and your niche's community.

Chapter 2:

CREATING VALUABLE CONTENT...FAST

Crafting valuable content that grabs the reader's attention is critical to getting returning readers, subscribers, and sales. At the same time, you need to complete the content creation stage so you can quickly move onto the content marketing stage—the critical stage for building a profitable content brand. This chapter will show you how to create valuable content faster so you have more time to promote the content that you create.

Have A Bias Towards Action

Creating valuable content at a faster rate starts with a mindset shift. In my Breakthrough Success interview with EOFire host John Lee Dumas, we touched upon taking action part in a conversation focused on building a podcasting empire. It was at this moment that JLD emphasized having a bias towards action.

During our interview, he explained having a bias towards action by saying, "So many people trick themselves into thinking that they need to wait for the perfect moment to happen...You need to have a bias towards action...not be afraid to make mistakes...just do things that scare you, and get you out of the comfort zone…and see where the chips will fall from there. That, to me, is the key to successful entrepreneurs."

The same individual who makes six figures every *month* from podcasting believes that a bias towards action is the key to successful entrepreneurs. You will make mistakes along the journey. Everyone does. With that said, if you are willing to go out of your comfort zone and turn action into your default choice, crafting valuable content will become an easier task that evolves into a fun activity.

Batch Your Content Production

During the same interview with JLD, he discussed how he batches his content production. Basically, he does all 30 interviews for his podcast over a 2-day period and gets interviewed on 20 podcasts on one day. This approach gives him 27 days to focus on other tasks for his content brand.

Ever since JLD mentioned the content batching method, I've noticed more and more people mention it. This is similar to when you buy a new car model and suddenly notice many of those car models on the road (there's even a name for this phenomena. It's called the Baader-Meinhof Phenomenon in case you're in the mood for a new trivia question).

All you may know about content batching is that JLD does it, but it's the secret to consistently creating valuable content with ease. Notice how JLD only spends two days each month interviewing people for his EOFire episodes. He also only spends one day getting interviewed for other podcasts.

While he takes on the herculean mission to consistently publishing one new episode every day, he's only working towards this herculean mission for two days each month. If you could grind for two days and then have all of your content completed and scheduled for that month, would you do it? And since most people don't publish daily podcast episodes, the content batching process is much easier for most of us.

If you write one blog post every other week and choose two days of the month to write 10 blog posts per day, you've got content scheduled for almost the entire year (I only recommend this approach if you have a solid promotional calendar in place, and even then you should leave some holes so you can insert new blog posts in case there's breaking news in your industry. For some niches, every day presents big news).

To get started with your content batching plan, choose a day of the week you'll conduct your content batching. For instance, you can choose Tuesdays to batch your content. You can also choose to exclusively batch your content on the first Tuesday of the month. The options available for your content batching are dependent on your schedule and the time you can commit to crafting valuable content. Since you'll have the ideas written in advance based on what you learned from Chapter 1, you won't get held back by a lack of ideas.

How To Craft Spectacular Content…FASTER

Crafting spectacular content comes down to providing a legendary experience for your targeted audience. Every time someone reads through a blog post, listens to a podcast episode, or watches a video, they have an experience. You want to make it legendary.

Spectacular blog posts, podcasts, and videos follow a similar recipe, but those recipes are slightly different due to the differences the distribution methods share. First, let's start with the core elements that all spectacular content (regardless of form) have in common.

#1: Attractive Headline: The headline determines how many of your readers will engage with your content from start to finish. If people don't like the headline, they will skip over your content. It is normal for me to write 10 headlines for a single piece of content before I decide on the winning headline. I need to get the bad ideas out of my system so I can find the headlines that will get the most attention and engagement for my content.

#2: Hooks The Reader: Your first sentence, regardless of whether that sentence is verbally or textually communicated, must hook the content consumer (i.e. reader, listener, viewer, etc.). Interesting questions, statistics, facts, and statements hook the consumer. That first sentence hooks them to read the rest of the paragraph, and it's that paragraph's job to hook the content consumer to engage with the rest of the content.

#3: The Body: This is where you share your insights or conduct the interview. In addition to sharing insights, you'll want to mention research and past content you've published. For instance, I had Trevor Oldham on Episode 40 my Breakthrough Success Podcast to discuss how we can ignite our motivation and productivity. During the episode, we got into a brief conversation about webinars, and I used that as a plug to mention the previous episode in which I talked with Jon Schumacher about using webinars to generate a massive profit. Don't only share great info within the body, but give your audience more ways to come in contact with your ideas and ideas from authority sites as well (both also help with SEO).

#3A: Make Your Body Skimmable: Most people will spend less than two minutes engaging with your content. They want to move onto the next task and get a sufficient amount of value from your content. If you give them this type of value, they'll come back for more. You must make it easy for your visitors to leave with all of the main points from your blog post in under two minutes. You do that with **bold text**, <u>underlined text</u>, and even *italicized text*. You can also accomplish the challenge with different sized text for names of tactics and/or colored text.

The only true way to make videos and podcast episodes skimmable is to time stamp the important parts of the video/episode. You can indicate the exact minute and second that you discuss a new topic or question. This allows your viewers and listeners to skip to their favorite parts of your videos/episodes.

#4: Ending With A Call-To-Action: At the end of your content, you need to summarize the content while providing a clear call-to-action. The CTA I use for my blog posts result in more comments and shares. For my podcast, my CTAs result in reviews, subscribers, and training course sales. My YouTube video CTAs result in more likes, comments, and subscribers.

The Stand Alone Factor

Those are the four basic elements of spectacular content regardless of the distribution method. The other critical element is to incorporate other media into your content. I include this element as a stand alone factor because the media you add to your content depends on the type of content you're utilizing.

For instance, blog posts can host a variety of medias including pictures and videos. It is advised to use one form of media for every 300 words. That way, your audience won't get bored by a wall of text and skim through the blog post from start to finish. With that said, the 300 word rule is just a benchmark that you can slightly exceed or fall short on depending on what you determine as the right call.

While pictures are the most popular form of media for blog posts, you should also incorporate YouTube videos, podcast episodes, and SlideShares whenever you can. Some people may skip over these forms of media, but when you get someone to watch the embedded video, podcast episode, or SlideShare, you are increasing the amount of time people spend on your site. In the long-term, search engines will greatly award you for your care towards this statistic.

When it comes to incorporating other forms of media, the best you can do with a podcast is to utilize the show notes where you can still follow the 300 word rule. During the episode, you can incorporate audio segments and your analysis of the interview afterwards. I rarely use this approach for my podcasts, but one approach I commonly use is mentioning other episodes. That way, I get listeners to engage with more of my episodes.

I will also reference videos and articles (whether written by me or not) and create short links that I mention during the episode. That way, people can use those links to access other media. It's the best way to incorporate the 300 word rule during the episodes, but I don't pay attention to it while conducting the interview. My focus is to deliver a legendary experience in the interview. I don't think about which episodes, videos, and articles I can mention, but if I think of them on the fly, I will mention them.

Create A Rubric Based On These Elements

Creating a rubric for your content creation will speed up the creation process. Not only will ideas flow more easily, but you also won't have to go back to these pages to figure out how to craft spectacular content.

I no longer need this list of elements in front of me when writing a blog post (or any form of content). That's because all of my blog posts follow a similar structure. They all have the hook, the body, and the conclusion that utilizes the CTA. The hooks and CTAs from different blog posts will sound similar if not identical.

My action step for you is to create a form of content using the elements of spectacular content. As you create this content, consciously become aware as you apply the elements into the content. If you are consciously aware of this action, repetition will become easier. Soon, you won't have to look back at your older content to structure your hook, body, and conclusion with the CTA.

Embrace The Efficiency Mindset

We all know efficiency is important. If you can perform the same task 30 minutes faster, you have 30 extra minutes to pursue new tasks. I don't believe everyone fully embraces efficiency to its highest potential.

I study the topic every day through my research and through my actions. I go VERY deep on the topic (I think of ways to put my clothing away in a shorter period of time, even if this only adds up to a few extra seconds) because all of those seconds and minutes add up. Plus, if you try to shave off seconds in a similar way, it won't take long before you shave off minutes or even hours of time from content completion while providing the same value.

Embracing efficiency is vital to creating valuable content at a faster rate. Think about how you can shave off one minute from the content creation process. Then think about how you can shave off two minutes from the content creation process. I'll give you some ideas and helpful hacks to get you started.

The Hack Of All Hacks For Content Creation

I'll start off with what is by far my favorite hack for content creation. I first learned about this hack from Jordan Baker, the CEO and lead developer of the Focuster App, an app which is designed to boost your productivity. When I asked him questions about boosting productivity during the Content Marketing Success Summit, he went into great detail about taking breaks, listening to the right music, and other productivity hacks.

However, Jordan unfolded the hacks of all hacks for content creators when he explained to me that he writes some of his blog posts on his smartphone.

This concept blew me away. Now, instead of awkwardly scrolling through my smartphone to pass the time while waiting (we have all been there), I can write a blog post, questions for an upcoming podcast interview, or outline my next video. In fact, I tried this while waiting in a clothing store and ended up writing a 1,000 word blog post. Who says shopping can't be productive?

Now I plan to incorporate this method any time I am waiting for something or someone. In the movie theater, instead of seeing advertisements of upcoming films, I can add more content to a blog post I am working on. You can take this approach a step further by verbally "writing" your blog post while driving the car and having your smartphone display the transcription (I haven't tried this yet. I prefer listening to audiobooks and podcast episodes during this time).

While most people associate content creation (blog posts in particular) with their computers, nothing is stopping you from using your smartphone to communicate and craft your ideas into distributable content.

Create A Schedule & Identify Your Standards

Creating a schedule and identifying your standards allows you to get clear on what work you need to put in for content creation every day.

When creating your standards, you must give yourself an activity that you can reliably do every day. If you want to start off easy on yourself to maintain the consistency, then do so, because consistency (or inconsistency) becomes a habit. In most cases, it is better to do a few things consistently than it is to do many things at an inconsistent rate. If you want to become a successful content creator, then you must be consistent in what you do.

Once you grow comfortable with being consistent in a few key areas, you must raise your bar higher. Success in content creation requires a leap out of the comfort zone, and by gradually leaping out of the comfort zone, you'll build the habits of raising your bar higher and rising up to challenges you'll encounter along the way.

Chapter 3:

YOUR ENVIRONMENT DETERMINES YOUR EFFICIENCY

Our environment affects us greatly, and mastering our environment is critical for us to master our productivity. How important is an environment? Ask a fish! If you put that fish in a fish bowl, it will swim around and await its food. If you put that same fish on the ground, it won't live very long. The same creature with the same genetic makeup was put into two different environments. In one environment, the fish is swimming happy. In the other environment, that same fish is struggling to breathe.

A change in your environment probably won't mean the difference between life and death. However, any change in your environment will subconsciously affect how you work and think. You won't see these gradual effects come into play. They'll just happen, and all of a sudden, you have submitted to your new environment.

We all submit ourselves to the environment we live in unless we decide to make a change. We'll talk more about making that change later, but let's start by defining an environment. An environment for our purposes isn't specifically a location. While location plays a role in defining our environment, the people we spend most of our time with are also a part of our environment. On the same college campus, there is one group of people who party every night and another group of people who do missionary work. Even though the location stays the same, the people in one group are completely different from the people who reside in the other group.

Now that we know what constitutes an environment, let's use that knowledge to create a more productive environment for our ambitions.

Anticipate Distractions

Distractions tempt us at every turn. When you go on the internet to grow your online business, the YouTube temptation looms nearby. When you walk near your TV, the temptation to start watching your TV grows within your soul. Even if you don't give up easily to surfing YouTube or turning on the TV, distractions are still everywhere. If you told me that you never check your inbox when you get new message, I'm waiting for the straight face to disappear. Notifications of new emails beg for our attention like puppies…and they win every time. We stop what we are doing just so that red circle indicating unread mail goes away.

While the inbox is a common distractor, I can't think of all of the possible ways we get distracted. I leave that up to you in the first step of creating a better environment for yourself. Each day, write down the things that distracted you and how long they distracted you for. If you want to solve any problem, you must identify the problem before doing anything else. Does your inbox take away most of your time? Is it the TV? Does surfing YouTube have your undivided attention?

Once you establish what distracts you each day, you must now anticipate those distractions and change the patterns that lead to those distractions. Here's where your environment starts to change. If you anticipate yourself watching TV, have a trustworthy person hide the remote. If you anticipate yourself opening your inbox, remove the mail icon from your dashboard. On my Mac Book Pro, a simple Force Quit on the Mail app gets the job done. I can always bring back my mail icon and check my mail by searching for the app within my dashboard. However, I won't get distracted by incoming mail when I'm writing a book. Anytime I see a distraction looming nearby, I change my environment to make it more difficult for myself to give into that distraction. If it's too difficult for me to distract myself, then I don't bother trying. The only option left is to focus more of my time, attention, and energy on my work.

Remove The Clutter

If you work at a desk, your desk is probably filled with distractions. Anything from a stack of papers to a disarray of folders can throw off your game. The only things you'll see on my desk are a pad of sticky notes, a piece of paper with my goals, motivational quotes, and sometimes a book which serves as motivation.

Working in a less cluttered environment will boost your productivity because a less cluttered environment gives you fewer things to randomly gaze at. When you have a stack of papers on your desk, it's easier to gaze off at those stacks of paper and get distracted. Any temporary distraction will hurt your productivity because each time you get distracted, it takes a certain amount of time to get back into the groove. If you incrementally add the occurrences of those 1-2 minutes it takes to get back into the groove, you'd be shocked with how much time you lose. If you get distracted in this manner three times per day, you lose about five minutes. Those are the five minutes that you didn't even realize you had until now. If you add that up for an entire year, you are distracted by clutter for a little over 30 hours every year. Imagine a time wizard showed up and gave you an extra 30 hours every year. What would you do with that time?

How To Create An Environment That Boosts Your Efficiency

Keeping clutter on your desk makes you more open to distraction. However, that's the least of your problems if you have a cluttered desk. That same cluttered desk will also prevent you from working more efficiently. If you have to search through a stack of papers to find what you're looking for, your efficiency will suffer over the long haul. Organize everything on your desk to make sure any piece of information is readily accessible. I like to organize this information and then move it to another room. While I like having this organized information, I don't want to gaze at it while I'm working and then let my mind wander any distance away from the current task.

A cluttered desk is far from the only thing within your environment. As I mentioned before, the people you spend most of your time with also reside within your environment. An easy way to boost your efficiency is to associate yourself with the people who will challenge you to accomplish more of your goals. It's easier for people to spend their time gossiping away with friends, host a pity party, and use excuses to make themselves feel better about not reaching their full potential. It's harder to make new friends and even harder to find friends who will motivate you to pursue your calling, but it's better to make new friends who will motivate you than keep the old friends who are holding you back.

You don't have to live nearby your friends. You can all interact continents away by using social media. Your best friends may not necessarily be a few minutes away. They may be a few hours away, but if you enjoy interacting with them and they motivate you, why not keep those friends? Those same friends can ignite you on your way to success.

Chapter 4:

TIME IS YOUR MOST VALUABLE RESOURCE

The way you use your time determines what results you get with your content brand, and to paint a bigger picture, the results you get in your life. We all have the same 24 hours in a given day, but some people focus most of those hours on productive tasks that lead to more revenue and awareness for their content brands.

If we could stop time and add extra hours to the day, it would be easier for us to build successful blogs, channels, and podcasts. While there's no way to pause time and work while everyone else is on pause, you can discover more time for yourself. You discover that extra time for yourself by outsourcing various tasks around you.

Chances are you do a variety of necessary tasks for your business that, although they are necessary, eat up your time. After you do all of those little tasks that keep you right where you are, you're too flustered to pursue the high priority tasks that will lead to your monumental growth. If you continue on this cycle, your content brand will stand still as time erodes away at methods that may no longer work or need a modified approach to achieve the same results. To avoid this stagnant cycle of constant but ineffective motion, you need to outsource your tasks to someone.

List Your Tasks

The first step to outsourcing more of your business is to list everything that you do. This step gives you clarity on what you do every day. List everything from writing blog posts to creating pictures. Once you create a list, put a big asterisk next to any task that you enjoy doing. See those tasks without the asterisks? Would you continue doing those tasks even if you were a billionaire, and you found perfect clones of yourself? Those are the tasks you need to start outsourcing. Don't wait until you have a lot of money in your pockets. You get the money by outsourcing various tasks and effectively utilizing your newfound time.

Getting The Right Freelancers

Once you list the tasks, it's time to start looking for freelancers. I personally use UpWork to hire my freelancers. Here are some of the tasks my freelancers take off my shoulders:

- Editing blog posts
- Editing podcast episodes
- Creating pictures
- Scheduling content
- Social media growth

I'll closely monitor a new freelancer for the first 1-2 weeks and continuously communicate with this freelancer. Once I trust the freelancer enough, I stop closely monitoring them unless a question pops up or there is a problem. I check on each of my freelancers weekly, and I check on some of my freelancers a little more depending on how much we communicate, but I don't micromanage. For people unfamiliar with the team, micromanaging is when you analyze every minute of your freelancer's work. You spend so much time analyzing their work that you forget to do the work you were meant to do with your newfound time. You didn't take any weight off your shoulders. You simply took one weight off your shoulders to replace it with an identical weight.

When I post a job, I look for freelancers who will be a valuable asset to my team, even if they charge a high price per hour. In most cases, low-priced freelancers won't get the job done as well. For ineffective freelancers, the end-result is you spending time fixing your freelancer's mistakes and continuously communicating with this freelancer to ensure the work is getting done all without seeing any progress towards more effectiveness and efficiency.

I then look at the application to determine past working experience and the cover letter to see if the freelancer understands what my job will entail. For a Twitter job, I turn away freelancers who spend much of their application talking about their SEO knowledge. I look for people who possess expertise in a specific area. I ignore the people who do a little bit of everything but are masters of none.

Within your proposal, you can include mandatory questions. Including the right questions will give you a better picture of each potential employee. Here are some good questions to ask:

- How would you describe your personality? — Know the person who's going to work for you. Is their personality the right fit?
- What movie did you watch recently? — This question turns the interview process into a conversation. You get an idea of what your freelancer does during off time and what kind of content they consume outside of work and how they interpret it.

- What did you like about your first job? — The answer to this question will help you create an enjoyable experience that yields greater productivity for your freelancer.
- What skills do you have that make you a perfect fit? — Get more specifics based on your job request so you know if the freelancer has the skills to perform your tasks.
- What have you done in the last 12 months to develop this skill? — This question lets you know how seriously your freelancer takes his/her work. Is the freelancer learning new insights or just getting by with his/her current knowledge.

What You Can Outsource

If you're not outsourcing, you are heading towards stagnancy. To get you started on some tasks you can start outsourcing, I compiled a list of tasks that may apply to you:

- Blog post editor
- Picture creation
- SEO
- Scheduling events in your calendar
- Social media posts
- Competitive research
- Book covers
- Research for each of your blog posts
- Responding to SOME emails sent your way
- Video uploads
- Descriptions
- Getting featured in the press
- Web design

- List of local events where you can speak at or sponsor
- Managing your freelancers

Those are 15 different ideas to scratch the surface. Some of these tasks apply specifically to you. Others won't apply to you right now, but some of those same tasks may apply to you later. Regardless of how many tasks you need to outsource, you need to address them all. Think about how different your results would be if you had to complete all 15 of those tasks on your own as compared to delegating all 15 of those tasks to freelancers. You'll have more time, and then it's up to you to use that time to generate more revenue.

Take The Path Of Least Resistance

When you make the transition from not working to putting in the work, you square off against resistance. Some people brush off resistance as if it never existed. Other people get conquered by resistance's wrath. The more resistance between you and the task ahead, the less likely you are to win that battle, even if you love doing your work.

If you love writing your books, but it takes 20 minutes for your computer to turn on, and half of your keyboard isn't working, you'll probably lose that battle to resistance (and need a new computer). On the other hand, if you turn on your computer and are instantly greeted by the full-screen draft of your upcoming book, and your computer is fine, it's much easier to start and finish writing your book.

At one point, I dreaded creating videos. I actually loved creating videos, but the resistance between me and a published video stretched far. For each video, I had to do the following:

- Come up with the video idea
- Construct the outline
- Put on a collared shirt
- Turn on the lights
- Set up the background (green backdrop)
- Start my computer
- Put the computer on the ironing board (that what I did when I was starting out)
- Mic up
- Open iMovie
- Begin recording
- Edit the videos on iMovie (iMovie comes with a lot of great features, but the editing was downright time consuming, especially with content batching in play)

I knew I couldn't continue producing videos with this level of resistance. It took me about 30 minutes just to prepare to make videos, and let's not even start with the editing. That's why I temporarily gave up on video. I saw some traction, but I didn't see a significant return just yet.

Even though I enjoyed doing videos, there was too much resistance between me and getting started with my work. Even if you have a high level of desire to perform a certain task, enough resistance will dramatically slow down or even stop you from performing that task.

Eventually, I decided to give video creation a second chance, but I also changed my environment so I could take the path of least resistance. Here's what I now do before I make new videos:

- Come up with the video idea
- Put on a collared shirt

- Turn on the lights
- Turn on two microphones
- Turn on the camera
- Begin recording
- Edit on ScreenFlow or QuickTime

This new approach eliminated several tasks and helped me complete other tasks faster. As I did more videos, I no longer felt a need to create an outline for every video idea. You could literally give me a video idea within my niche right now, and if you gave me five seconds to think it over, I could probably create a five minute video. That type of transformation happens with daily practice.

Before this change, I actually used KeyNote presentations for some of my videos, and it was time consuming (as was the rest of the process before I changed my approach). Now I just turn on my camera, and that takes out the process of getting my computer, turning it on, going to iMovie, and getting started. I also no longer need the green backdrop since I do my videos in front of a white wall. My chair and desk are also set up for me in advance. I just leave them in the same spot after I finish creating videos for the day.

In your journey, you'll face resistance, but that's different from creating resistance for yourself by making it more difficult for you to pursue the work that you love doing. By making the change to my video preparation, I reduced the amount of self-inflicted resistance between me and my work. Reducing the amount of self-inflicted resistance between you and your work, no matter how big or small, will make it easier for you to pursue the work that matters. The easier it is for you to pursue the work that matters, the easier it will be for you to boost your productivity and get the results you want.

Outsource Your Way To ZERO Resistance

No matter how efficient your process becomes, you'll still square off with some resistance. I've created a strategy to write blog posts as efficiently as possible. However, I still don't like editing them; I never have.

Instead of embracing blog post editing, I decided to create another option. I decided to outsource blog post editing to a freelancer. That same freelancer even schedules the blog posts for me in advance. Now there's less resistance between me and a published blog post. All I have to do is write the blog post and send it off to my freelancer. The pictures are provided for me in advance by another freelancer.

Outsourcing some of my tasks shaves off at least 30 minutes of time for each blog post I publish. While my blogging frequency is increasing, I made this change when I only published 1 blog post per week. That's 52 blog posts each year that I save 30 minutes on. I save 26 hours every year by outsourcing this work. If you added up all of the tasks I outsource to freelancers, I easily save at least 1 month every year by outsourcing some of the tasks that were necessary but not desirable for me to do. Just because something is necessary for the survival of your business doesn't mean its necessary for you to do. The CEOs of big corporations aren't doing all of the work. Sure, they are highly productive, but they hire many employees to get various tasks accomplished. These CEOs even hire managers to ensure the employees are doing their work effectively and efficiently. They delegate as much as possible, and so should you.

Outsourcing more of your tasks will open up countless hours for you to pursue new opportunities. By setting up your environment to boost your productivity, you'll get more accomplished by outsourcing your work. At this point, chances are you have two questions for me:

- What should I outsource?
- How do I pay for this?

Let's start with what you would outsource. To begin, start by writing down everything that you do. Then, identify what you enjoy doing. Put a star next to anything that you enjoy doing. Everything else needs to get outsourced over time. The first task you should outsource is the most time consuming task. Outsourcing this task to someone will open up more time than outsourcing any other task. You can truly reap the benefit of the extra time.

While outsourcing sounds good in theory, the costs will grow as you introduce more freelancers to your team. It won't take long before you pay hundreds and even thousands of dollars for your freelancers' service each month. When you outsource your first task, utilize that extra time and see what happens before outsourcing anything else. You want to outsource gradually. You don't want to give yourself a sudden increase in costs. Sudden, dramatic increases in your costs are more difficult to keep up with. Then you'll find yourself struggling to pay off your freelancers. Don't let that be you.

The best way to continue hiring freelancers without worrying about costs is to assess how you utilize your extra time. If you hire someone to work 10 hours each week at a rate of $8/hr, then you need to make at least $80 every week with those extra 10 hours to keep that freelancer on your team (or the freelancer does work that brings in at least $80/week for your business). Even if you only break even, the freelancer is still a valuable asset to your team (unless your objectives change or you are micromanaging and therefore aren't utilizing your newfound time correctly). You can then outsource another task and see if you make a profit with the extra time. As long as a freelancer's work indirectly or directly helps you break even or make a profit, that freelancer can stay on your team.

Avoid Over Expansion

At this stage of the game, you may be eager to hire as many freelancers as possible. I need you to resist this temptation. If you hire too many freelancers too quickly, keeping up with their payroll will be a challenge. You'll soon run out of revenue that way. You only reap the true benefits of outsourcing if you gradually add to your freelancer army. To understand this logic, you need to understand the additional purpose of outsourcing.

Outsourcing's core purpose is to create more time in your day. You pay a certain amount of money to continue outsourcing any given task. To make your outsourcing efforts worthwhile, you must make more money with your extra time than you spend to create that extra time. That sentence is worth repeating. **To make your outsourcing efforts worthwhile, you must make more money with your extra time than you spend to create that extra time.** Once you make more money with your extra time than you spend to create that extra time, you can then approach the next freelancer.

You'll never finish what you don't start. Every finisher once stood at the starting line. The content creators you admire went through the same journey you're going through now. We all have our different backstories, but we also have a shared dream of building our own content brand empires that empower and/or entertain our audiences. Normally a paragraph like this gets used to motivate people to get started with their blog, channel, and/or podcast. However, I see this as a new beginning for all of us that we need to fully embrace.

Chapter 5:

AVOIDING OVERWHELM

Right now, you may feel excited about creating content. After listening to all of the speakers at the Content Marketing Success Summit, that's exactly how I felt. The summit inspired me to write this book, more training courses, and more products and services in general. It also inspired me to craft more content.

However, with increased content creation, content marketing, and product creation comes the risk of overwhelm. While we love our work, the same work we love so much can lead us to disaster. Let me provide a brief illustration.

The blogger enjoys writing blog posts. That blogger then decides to do weekly videos and podcast episodes to increase her means of distribution. This blogger must also find time in her day to promote her content and create products so she can support herself from her content brand. With a never ending stream of work, this blogger relationships with important people in her life may get damaged. If we work for over 10 hours every day, how much time do we have to build relationships and enjoy ourselves outside of work? Are we alert and alive or exhausted and burnt out during that time?

The risk of overworking is that you fall into a weird space where you want to do anything other than what you're currently doing. If you spend time with family and friends or doing a hobby, you're thinking, "I could be working right now." If you spend time working, you're thinking, "I need to strengthen my relationships with my family and friends right now. That's what I should be doing with my time."

If you feel overwhelmed while writing blog posts, creating videos, or interviewing a guest for your upcoming podcast episode, the overwhelm will show. Earlier in Chapter 4, we briefly discussed outsourcing, and while I believe this is a great overwhelm reducer, we still need to address the work we currently perform and don't want to outsource right now.

For instance, I write at least 1,000 words in a given day to stay sharp on my writing. That's something I won't outsource. I also enjoy conducting the podcast interviews. I take great pleasure in conducting the interviews. In this case, I can outsource finding guests for my podcasts, but I'll never outsource the interviews to someone else. For my podcast episodes and summit sessions, I am the host. I enjoy the privilege of interviewing hundreds of leaders within my niche, asking questions, learning from them, and sharing their insights with my audience.

I won't go into an exhaustive discussion on outsourcing because we already covered that. This chapter is for those tasks like hosting your own podcast episodes and writing 1,000 words every day—the tasks you don't want to outsource to anyone.

Create An Advanced Schedule

For a very long time, I would get out a sticky note each night and write down tomorrow's tasks. If I had to write a blog post tomorrow, I'd write that task on my sticky note. This is a popular tactic for remembering your tasks and waking up with the right frame of mind. However, it is a flawed approach.

I keep all of my sticky notes in envelops. I can go back to the sticky notes where I wrote tasks for the following:

#1: Content Marketing Success Summit (June 2017)

#2: *Lead The Stampede* (my first 200+ page book, published in 2014).

#3: Some stuff from my junior year of high school (I don't miss the SAT one bit)

I have many sticky notes that I use, but now I barely touch them. I only use them for spur of the moment ideas that I need to get out of my mind so I can focus on the task in front of me.

But what about writing tomorrow's tasks the night before? When you write these tasks on the sticky notes, you'll remember them. However, that system is flawed.

In his book, *The Ultimate Sales Machine*, Chet Holmes recommends creating a schedule of your entire day the night before. This is completely different from listing everything you need to do the night before. Not only do you list the tasks you must complete tomorrow, but you also give a time stamp for when you'll start and when you'll stop. For instance, I use the mornings to write content for my books and blog posts.

Here's what one day in my 2017 summer schedule looked like:

8:00 am Wake Up

8:30 am — 9:15 am — Run

9:15 am — 9:30 am — Shower

9:30 am to 10:00 am — Eat & Get Ready

10:00 am — 12:00 pm — Write book

12:00 pm — 1:00 pm — Contact potential summit speakers

1:00 pm — 2:00 pm — Create videos

2:00 pm — 3:00 pm — Respond to emails and freelancers

3:00 pm — 3:15 pm — Create show notes rubric for a freelancer

3:15 pm — 4:15 pm — Run

4:15 pm — 5:00 pm — Bike

5:00 pm — 5:45 pm — Shower & Eat

5:45 pm — 6:30 pm — Contact podcasts

6:30 pm — 7:00 pm — Summit preparation

7:00 pm — 8:00 pm —Write guest post

8:00 pm — 8:30 pm — Plan out webinars

8:30 pm — 9:00 pm — Plan out next free gift and the funnel

9:00 pm — 9:30 pm — Read

9:30 pm Bed

Creating this schedule the night before eliminates choice. For a very long time, I didn't have to worry about what I needed to do. Now, I no longer worry about *when I need to do what I have to do.*

Tomorrow's schedule will look similar in some ways but completely different in other ways. I always start the day with a run, but I may write a blog post instead of responding to emails and freelancers. I may also have some interviews for my Breakthrough Success Podcast

If you give yourself too many choices (i.e. should I write the book or create videos now?), you'll chip away at your willpower. It didn't take much willpower to write this book. On some days, I wrote from 10:00 am to 12:00 pm. On other days, I wrote from 3:00 pm to 5:00 pm. Regardless of when I started writing, I knew when I had to write content for this book. Eliminating the questions "What should I do?" and "When should I do it?" the night before will work wonders for your productivity.

The Work-Life Balance

I have heard many arguments for and against the work-life balance. Some entrepreneurs say you need to grind for 14 hours every day when you've got a startup. Others say 14 hours each day isn't enough. Just to mix things up more, there's a group of entrepreneurs who advocate for five hour workdays. Some people believe the work-life balance is nonexistent. The work-life balance definitely exists, but not in the way most people think.

Pro balancers say that the time you take off from your work allows you to increase your productivity when you're actually working. The idea is that taking breaks boosts your energy, and that extra energy allows you to more effectively utilize your time. If you overwork, you'll get to the point where working for two hours equates to the same productivity as one hour. You're only productive for every other minute if you become a workaholic.

My philosophy of the work-life balance is an imbalance that averages out as a balance. If you look at my schedule from earlier, you'll notice that most of the day is committed towards work. Not much of a life balance there. Normally, I have some free space where I take a break and do some activities with my family.

However, I created this schedule just after our 3-day vacation at Boston. During this three day period, I did very little work. At the very most, I remember contacting 20 potential speakers for my summit and reading 70 pages from a book I just got at an Amazon Bookstore. I added 11 high performance and business books to my collection, so I'll desperately tally that for the work section.

During that 3-day vacation, we went to two Boston Red Sox games (including the game when Big Papi's number got retired). The Red Sox went 1-1 during our visit. We also went to a few shopping centers where I got some books (I prefer spending my money on books than virtually anything else), Chipotle, and, of course, smoothies. After taking a 3-day vacation from my work, I needed to get back to speed. My mother and brother are also entrepreneurs so I wasn't the only one with this type of schedule.

On some days, I'll completely focus on my work. On other days, I'll completely focus on life outside of work. Work is a critical part of my life that provides me a strong sense of purpose, so I refuse to draw a line between work and life as they coexist with each other.

Drawing that line is the biggest mistake you can possibly make because you'll resent your work since, based on that line, your work has nothing to do with your life. You'll just view work as a burden you must complete in order to live out the rest of your life. However, this worldview will ooze into the other areas of your life. Irritation at work carries over to relationships and any free time that you get. If you love your work, you'll love your life. You can replace the word "love" with any word, like despise, and the same will be true.

I loved having the privilege of writing this book, hosting the Content Marketing Success Summit, and having the ability to create more content. I don't view each video as another task I need to do to make some extra income so I can move on to the "life side." I view content creation as a privilege which is based on the value I provide and the ability to turn my efforts into revenue.

You view your work as a duty that you have the privilege of fulfilling for your audience. You don't have to do your work. You get the privilege to do your work.

How To Take Breaks

I like to view the work-life balance as a work-break balance. You put in the work, but taking breaks is necessary for refueling your energy. However, if you take the wrong breaks, you'll feel exhausted, over extend your break, and the work will seem to drag on.

When I started on my entrepreneurial journey, video games were my quick choice for a break. I played them well before I became an entrepreneur, and this was long before I took my fitness as seriously as I take it now. There was no hesitation as I wandered over to the GameCube, Wii, or Wii U depending on what I felt like using at the time. Super Smash Bros or Mario Kart…every time.

Most of the time, I played video games longer than I should have. When I got back to work, I often thought of how long I had to work before I could resume playing video games. This infinite loop continued for a while. Eventually, I got better at managing the time I spent playing video games. Then, I accidentally stumbled across a monumental shift.

This monumental shift struck during a vacation. I can't explain why, but I decided on that vacation to give up video games so I could play the piano. I didn't bring any video games with me to vacation, so I had a two week buffer. That two week buffer was enough to eliminate my video game habit. I unplugged the video games before I did my share of unpacking the car. I made the change before any thoughts of, "I want to play video games" could resurface.

Now that I've shared my transformation story of eliminating a negative cornerstone habit from my life (we'll explore habits very soon), let's discuss taking the right breaks. During any break you take, *you must be active*. If you are watching your favorite TV shows, you are passive. You are watching life pass by without creating a legacy that others pass on. I know that's a brutal viewpoint of watching TV, but it's my viewpoint. I only watch TV for 4 hours every week, and when I watch TV, I only watch when the rest of the family is watching. The only thing TV is good for is bringing the entire family together, but it's better to think of more creative ways to bring the family together than watching TV.

My active breaks consist of reading, exercising, and playing the piano. I exercise 2-3 times in a given day. I read 30 books in a given month. I mostly replay previous songs I learned on the piano but aim to learn one new song on the piano every month. All of these breaks are active. I do not passively watch TV, surf through YouTube, or find myself browsing through the trending topics.

The best breaks are the active ones that boost your creativity and/or allow you to reconnect with your family and friends. A trip to the restaurant with your family may not fire up your brain cells with new information, but you'll feel a sense of belonging and fulfillment when you spend that time with your family. That sense of belonging and fulfillment will inspire you to produce greater work.

We must carefully select the tasks we perform in any given day, but we must also carefully select when we take breaks, how often we take the breaks, and what we do during those breaks. Every two hours I spend writing this book, I read a book for 30 minutes. This habit of reading a book for 30 minutes gives me a dopamine rush that allows me to approach my work with more vigor while the new knowledge flowing through my mind. I usually spend considerable time with my family and friends in the early evening when my productivity tends to drop anyway. Mornings are untouchable as I am highly productive in the early hours of the day. Your habits will determine what you do during these times of the day.

How Habits Get Formed

We have all developed life-changing habits. The question is whether those habits are serving you or hurting you. In most cases, you can barely see the effects habits have on your life, but their effects on your life are powerful. In his book *The Power Of Habit*, Charles Duhigg notes that "though each habit means relatively little on its own, [they] have enormous impacts on our health, productivity, financial security, and happiness."

Duhigg also conducted research on how habits happen. Here's the three steps to any habit's implementation:

1. Cue—something that triggers a behavior to begin (i.e. seeing your computer may trigger you to turn that computer on)
2. Routine—what happens after receiving the cue (i.e. opening the computer and logging in)
3. Reward—the final result. (i.e. being logged in and having the power to use your computer)

Knowing the three step process that forms all habits makes it possible to amplify certain habits that we want in our lives, such as writing habits that allow us to write better blog posts. The next time you read a book or write more content, ask yourself what the cue for your action was. What triggered you to take your course of action? How do you feel about the reward? Can you make yourself feel better about the reward of writing content or reading a book so you perform those actions more often?

Having clarity about how something happens makes it easier to reach a solution and perform that same activity more effectively.

Assess Your Current Habits

Now that you know how habits get formed, it's time to use this advice to our advantage. Assessing your current habits comes down to identifying which habits are serving you and which habits are hurting you. Write them down. Think back to how and why you developed these habits. I developed the habit of writing 1,000 words per day because I love writing.

However, I also learned of a game people play where if they fail to implement a task that they want to develop into a habit, they donate X dollars to an anti-charity. I couldn't see myself making this kind of donation, so that fear also keeps me in check. Ever since I read about this game some people play, I've never missed a day of writing at least 1,000 words in a given day unless I intentionally take the entire day off.

For some of your bad habits, you may need to challenge yourself that way. I use my vacations to break my bad habits as it's a complete change in scenery that completely removes most of the cues from existence. Without consciously being aware of how powerful vacation are, I'd still be playing video games every day. My business would have stayed right where it was.

You may not have the luxury of a two week vacation. However, you have the luxury of a library, a coffee shop, and other places where you can remove yourself from the typical cues of your home or workplace. You'll hear many stories of writers working in the library or the coffee shop because these two environments remove the distractions of the home such as the TV remote and socializing.

While I believe people should socialize with their families every day, you need to set some boundaries to get your best work done. I write my content at home, but I typically write my content very early in the day. I'm the only one awake when I start writing content for my book, blog post, or whatever I'm working on. I wait a few hours before I start creating videos and interviewing people because I respect my family members' sleeping hours.

Tampering with the cue, routine, and reward will also help you eliminate bad habits that are holding you back. It's helpful to ask questions like, "How am I holding myself back?" instead of questions like, "What's holding me back?" to get more clear on what you can do to drive change.

Identify What Habits You Want In Your Life

Once you have assessed the habits that guide or derail your life, it's time to identify the habits you want in your life. Start thinking of what habits would help you the most in your personal and professional life. Writing 1,000 words and reading for an hour every day are both great starting point for bloggers and authors.

When you develop a habit, you want to start off with a small barrier of entry. I could attempt to develop the habit of writing 20,000 words every day, but achieving this habit would be far too stressful. I would have to pause many of my existing habits—even the good ones—so I could achieve this goal. I've written as much as 15,000 words in a given day, but I don't write that many words every day.

I prefer setting 1,000 words per day as the minimum. At the end of a given day, I sometimes write 2,000 to 3,000 words which puts me in a position to write 60,000 to 90,000 words every month. That alone is 1-2 books and some blog posts.

You need to create daily habits for content creation and promotion that match up with your method(s) of content distribution. If you have a podcast, you should contact a certain number of potential guests each day. Don't outsource that part as a podcast allows you to build amazing relationships. If you have a YouTube channel, create a certain number of videos every day. Publish some of those videos on your YouTube channel and save others for a training course.

One Powerful Content Creation Habit

I recently read Tom Corson-Knowles' book *The Kindle Publishing Bible*. In addition to learning how to win in the Kindle landscape, I learned about a powerful writing habit. While this habit can be applied to video production and podcasting, this habit especially resonates with writing. The reason most writers don't become authors or successful bloggers is because they fear imperfection. No matter how much effort you put into your book or blog post, you'll find a reason to believe it's not ready.

The habit Tom Corson-Knowles uses to write and publish his content at a rapid pace (he's published over 25 books) is frictionless publishing. Here's how Tom describes frictionless publishing in his book:

> "For frictionless publishing, I write the book, finish the chapters and then post it on Kindle with minimal or no editing immediately for 99 cents. At this stage, the book is definitely worth at least 99 cents so I know that anyone who reads it will get a lot of value out of it and will NOT be disappointed in their investment."

He got the idea of frictionless publishing from Leo Babauta, founder of the Zen Habits blog. Leo originally suggested frictionless blogging which is frictionless publishing but for a blog post. You publish your blog post before it's actually done. Since the world can see that blog post, you'll get more productive and quickly make the final changes since incoming visitors will see the unfinished content. Just make sure your blog post is valuable enough to be worthy of someone's time…even though it's unfinished.

You'll never feel ready to hit the publish button. You'll always see something wrong with your content, and that's fine…as long as you publish it. Always seeing something wrong with your content and never publishing it is letting the poisonous desire for perfection drag you down to the depths.

Frictionless publishing has become even easier for videos and podcast episodes. If you broadcast the videos and podcast episodes live, then you eliminate the need for editing, uploading the video or audio file to a server, and scheduling it for release. For some people, the post-creation process is a tedious process that is easier to skip over. I've even outsourced certain parts of the post-creation such as uploading videos and scheduling content for release because the post-creation process is very tedious for me.

This is why I love the concept of frictionless publishing. You don't have to worry too much about the post-creation process. In the case of publishing a book or blog post, you'll have an amazing sense of urgency to edit what you created (that's a good problem to have).

Recharging Your Body

Our ability to produce meaningful content and spread our messages comes down to three critical factors. In *The Productivity Project*, Chris Bailey refers to time, attention, and energy as the key determinants of productivity. We understand the concept of time. Put in more time and effort, and we *should* get more results.

Apply attention to one task at a time, and we no longer work distracted. When I write content for books and blog posts, I write that content so early in the day that looking in my inbox actually bothers me. Later in the day, the inbox doesn't bother me and I must resist the urge to check my inbox, but in the morning, there is no urge to check my inbox. At 5:30 am, I am not interested in engaging in multiple conversations and figuring out how I need to respond (and then responding to follow-ups). At that time, I am either running or writing content for my book.

Energy is a chief component of productivity that most people ignore. If you feel sluggish, then it doesn't matter how many hours you spend crafting your content. That's why I incorporate small breaks throughout the day that allow me to feel recharged. Even if you can "productively" work with a sluggish body, you'll be so much more productive if you give your body the proper recharge. That begins with breaks, but breaks will only recharge your body so much.

Take Naps!

For a very long time, I strongly opposed naps. Now I'm a believer. By lying in my bed for 20 minutes, I give my body just enough time to rest but not too much time to get comfortable. This is an important distinction because if you nap too long, you'll actually feel worse than if you hadn't napped at all (you risk waking up when your body is deep in its 1.5 hour sleep cycle).

I enjoy waking up early in the morning because it provides an unparalleled sense of productivity. However, I also enjoy taking naps in the middle of the day to avoid slugging through the rest of the day. I wake up very early in the morning to write content even if I feel as if I didn't get the best sleep. After I write the content, I'll take my break to read a book and then take my 20 minute nap. I'll read first because my eyes were just exposed to the blue light of the computer screen. Reading is productive and allows my eyes some time away from the blue light before I begin my nap. I also remedy this effect by wearing blue light repellent glasses which reflect the blue light away from my eyes. I only use these glasses very early or very late into the day, so don't expect to see me walking around with them on.

I like to schedule my naps in the middle of the day, especially at times when I know I am the least productive. For instance, my productivity is low at 3 pm. At that time, I will either nap or schedule an interview as scheduling an interview forces me to be productive while napping gives me a recharge that boosts my productivity for other tasks.

What You Put In Determines What You Get Out

My mother is a nutritionist, and I have food allergies, so I pay special attention to what I put in my body. As a side note, she switched from her Goldman Sachs job to being a nutritionist because I was very sick at a very early age and she did everything in her power to get me to where I am today.

One of the lessons the Guberti family knows very well is that what you put into your body determines what you get out. It's easy to tell who's eating the junk food too much and who's living the healthy lifestyle (we live the healthy lifestyle, but we can determine who isn't living a healthy lifestyle. If you don't believe we eat healthy, just check my mom's Instagram where she often takes pictures of what we eat). If you eat unhealthy foods, you'll feel more sluggish and won't be the ideal person to spend time with. If you eat healthier foods, you'll feel more energetic (or you have too much caffeine intake).

This is why I rarely eat sugary foods. Anytime I eat sugar, I know my productivity drops. Anytime I consider the occasional chocolate bar, I hunt for the option with under 10 grams of sugar and some protein. I've never consumed a Hershey's or Snickers bar because my allergies forbid it (even if I didn't have allergies, try slipping one of those bars into the kitchen with a nutritionist who can rattle off at least 10 reasons in 60 seconds why those bars are bad for you).

Commit yourself to eliminating the junk food from your life. Remember that you've only got one life. Junk food won't kill you now, but it's robbing you of meaningful time. Imagine stuffing junk food down your body and then writing 1,000 words, creating the five videos, or interviewing someone for your podcast. Just thinking of that makes me cringe.

Every time you decide to consume food, ask yourself how this will affect your short-term and long-term performance. Eating junk food once will negatively impact your short-term performance. Continuously eating junk food will negatively impact your long-term performance until you stop eating the junk food. If you know an activity will negatively impact your short-term and/or long-term performance without any upside, it shouldn't even be considered. Just to be clear, I measure performance based on my ability to thrive during my self-assigned working hours and to play harder with my family and friends. If I can do one but not the other, I need to fix my performance.

Get clear on what high performance means to you, and make sure the foods and drinks you put into your body support that vision. What we put into our bodies significantly impacts our output in our personal lives and professional lives. What are you putting into your body?

Chapter 6:

OPTIMIZING YOUR CONTENT FOR SUCCESS

With the productivity portion of the book complete, we'll now head towards the final portion of the content creation part of the book. It doesn't take long to discover that creating valuable content isn't enough. You can't publish content, hope it will rank high on Google, and then do nothing about it.

When you master valuable content creation, you master writing the type of content that attracts people to your content and keeps their attention. Creating valuable content helps, but without the marketing, your content will be the greatest kept secret.

The two optimization goals for your content are to optimize for search engines and social shares. At the same time, you must craft content focused on the reader. If you stuff keywords and share buttons without providing your audience with a legendary experience, they won't stick around. That's why I shared the framework for crafting spectacular content back in Chapter 2. Now we optimize that content so people share it.

In this book, content optimization is categorized as content creation as opposed to content marketing because you optimize the content first and then attract the audience. That way, once you attract the audience, you'll get more of your visitors to share your content with their social media audiences.

We'll start with boosting social shares and then dive into SEO.

Why People Share Content And What That Means For Your Content

If you can understand why people share content and which content they like to share within your niche, then you can craft contagious blog posts that would be so enticing that most of your visitors will share your blog post to their social media audiences. As more people share your blog posts with their social media audiences, your reach will expand, and you will reach visitors and customers that you could not have reached with your own efforts.

In a study conducted by *The New York Times* about why people share content, 94% of respondents said that they carefully consider how the information they share will be of use to other people. 84% of respondents said that they share content that supports special causes or issues that they care about. A different study confirmed that the three main reasons people share content is because they find it interesting, they think the content is helpful, and they want want to make people laugh. According to Social Triggers, positive content outperforms negative content.

So in other words, positive, helpful, entertaining, and humorous content wins. Not every content topic can exemplify all four of these characteristics, but when you craft your content, you should always strive to combine at least three of these four characteristics together, and preferably, all four of the characteristics should exist in the same piece of content.

You can craft helpful content and add a humorous joke or two related to the topic. You can use a personal experience, an experience shared by many, a common fact that we all know to be true, or a clever twist from a common way of thinking. Sometimes you can combine multiple characteristics in a single sentence. The example below is a combination of helpfulness (valuable tidbit) and humor. You could also argue that it fits the descriptions of positive and entertaining.

"Dear Realist, Optimist, and Pessimist—

While you guys were busy arguing whether the glass is half full or half empty, I sold the glass.

Sincerely,

Entrepreneurist"

Obviously, this quote has a focus on humor. Occasionally including humorous pictures or jokes in the middle of helpful content will engage the visitor in a new way, and that visitor will find himself/herself engaging with more of your content to find helpful tidbits and humorous jokes along the way.

I have seen hundreds of public speakers talk about business and entrepreneurship at events. We all have a natural tendency to like some people more than others and have our #1 role model on the top of the list. Now recollecting on all of the events I ever attended, the public speakers who combined positivity, value, entertainment, and humor into their speeches are the same speakers who found themselves towards the top of my list.

Just think about if one of those elements is missing from your content. If positivity is missing, we might laugh and be entertained, but we don't leave feeling empowered or any better about ourselves. Without value, your content will fail to serve your audience. Without entertainment, your content can provide a lot of value but risk boring people. Incorporating humor makes it easier for people to remember you, and if you take your content seriously, you want people to remember that content.

Out of all four of these cornerstones, I focus on value. Some of my content only features one joke while I'll incorporate several jokes into some of my other content. Providing value is the core focus.

Getting People To Share Your Content

You could create content that possesses all four elements, but if you make it difficult for people to share your content, then your pieces of content won't get shared. Without social sharing buttons at the top or bottom of your content, your content brand will have an increasingly difficult time spreading on social media.

It is an unnecessary burden to place on yourself primarily because on most blogging services such as WordPress, it is easy to include social sharing buttons at the bottom of every blog post. For a WordPress blog, all you have to do is go to "Settings—> Share" in the dashboard to choose which social networks people can use to share your content. You can write blog posts that focus on your videos, podcast episodes, or any other type of content.

Although it is powerful to put social sharing buttons at the bottom of every blog post, you don't want to get consumed by the power. Some people choose to add dozens of social media icons at the bottom of their blog posts. Remember that the more social sharing options you provide your visitors with, the more difficult it is for the visitor to choose the 1-2 social sharing buttons to click and then share your content on.

As of writing, I only use four social sharing buttons for my blog which allow people to easily share my content on Twitter, Facebook, LinkedIn, and Pinterest. If I really wanted to, I could have included 10 other social networks, but then the popular options (Twitter, Facebook, etc) would be crowded by the not as popular options.

The more social sharing options you provide, the more you'll overwhelm your visitors. The more overwhelmed your visitors are by the sharing options, the less likely they are to share your content.

Optimizing Your Content For Social Shares

Utilizing social sharing buttons is a great start towards optimizing your content for social shares. However, you are trusting that people scroll all the way to the bottom of your content. If you include social sharing buttons at the top of your content, you must trust that your visitors will scroll back to the top after consuming your content or share your content based on preexisting trust.

Luckily, there is a middle ground that actually acts as the high ground. Embedding social sharing buttons throughout your content gives your visitors the power to share your content at any moment in the consumption process. It's far easier to do this with a blog than any other form of content. Several plugins and tools will help you create links that lead to prewritten messages to tweet, post on Facebook, and share on other social networks.

My recommendation for audio content is to provide a show notes link and include the sharing buttons there, similarly to a blog post. You can also create a custom link which leads to a bunch of prewritten posts for various social networks, but I advise simply leading people to the show notes so they can more easily consume additional content.

For videos, you can use the beginning of the video to ask for shares if they enjoy it and do the same thing at the end of the video. I prefer to ask for comments, likes, and subscribers as that will boost my YouTube video's ranking. You can also ask for shares in the description of your video and even embed your videos into your blog posts. That way, when the blog post gets shared, your video picks up some exposure as well.

Now, how do you place sharing buttons in different points of your content? You can use Click To Tweet to generate prewritten tweets so all people need to do is click on the link and then click "Tweet." This free tool allows you to turn any part of your blog post into an opportunity for people to share your content via social media.

I craft the prewritten messages when I review my content before publication. During a review, I look for particularly effective tidbits of knowledge that people would want to tweet...but only if that call-to-action was presented to them. Click To Tweet allows me to present the call-to-action. My visitors get enticed to tweet certain sentences from my blog post. When I want to use a Click To Tweet link, I simply put "[Click To Tweet]" at the end of the sentence with a link to the tweet. This lets visitors know that by clicking the link, they can tweet out my sentence.

You can use a tool called Sumo to get a similar effect for both Facebook and Twitter.

I only review written content in this format. For videos and podcasts, I'll have my editor write down some quotes from the episode or video that I can use for prewritten social sharing options. Sprinkle the sharing buttons sparingly throughout your content. Your visitors don't engage with your content with the sole purpose of sharing it. If your content fulfills your visitor's goal (i.e. does the video/post/episode give them clarity on their content marketing strategy), they'll be more inclined to share your content. Sprinkling the sharing buttons throughout your content is the icing on the cake.

Optimizing Your Blog Posts For Search Engines

While you can see some short-term social media results that lead to long-term prosperity, you'll rarely see any short-term results from your SEO strategy. With that said, the long-term potential for SEO traffic greatly outweighs the long-term potential for social media traffic.

Social media traffic is a means of acquiring short-term traffic that can turn into quality long-term traffic given that you're growing your social media audience. SEO takes more time in the beginning, but the end result is worth the wait.

We'll go more into detail about SEO during the Content Marketing part of the book. However, part of SEO specifically revolves around content creation and matters that are outside of the content marketing realm. We'll talk about that side of SEO now.

Why Blog Speed Is Crucial For SEO And Your Blog's Success

Blog speed is increasingly gaining influence in how search engines rank our blogs. Faster blogs tend to rank higher than slower blogs because Google wants a quick transition between a link click and the visitor seeing the content they expect to see.

Normally, a blog loads in a few seconds. Before our world got so fast, it would be acceptable for something to take a few seconds. Now, each extra second it takes for a blog to load is not as accepted. For every second it takes for a blog to load, page abandonment increases. If it takes more than four seconds to load, then 25% of your visitors will abandon your page before reading any of your content.

Blog speed also affects shopping behavior, and having a slow blog will decrease the likelihood of you getting customers. Here are some telling statistics from KISSmetrics that indicate how important blog speed is for customer behavior:

- 47% of consumers expect a web page to load in 2 seconds or less
- 79% of shoppers who are dissatisfied with website performance are less likely to buy from the same site again
- 52% of online shoppers state that quick page loading is important to their site loyalty
- A one second delay (or three seconds of waiting) decreases customer satisfaction by about 16%
- 44% of online shoppers will tell their friends about a bad experience online
- A one second delay in page response can result in a 7% reduction in conversions

These statistics make it clear that blog speed is not just important for search engines, but blog speed also determines what type of experience visitors have when they visit your blog. If your blog is fast, visitors will be more likely to stay loyal to your brand, but every extra second it takes for your website to load can have disastrous consequences. In the fast paced world we find ourselves in today, every second counts!

How To Make Your Blog Load Faster

No matter how slow or fast your blog loads, a faster blog will help you attract visitors who stay on your blog for a longer period of time. There are several easy-to-do fixes that will allow your blog to load faster:

1. **Have fewer blog posts on each page on your blog**. When someone goes to your blog, it takes time to load each blog post. The more blog posts you have on one page of your blog, the longer it will take for your blog to load. I used to have 15 blog posts on each page, and it took a very long time for my blog to load. Ever since I decided to only show five blog posts per page, my blog has loaded faster since there is less content that needs to get loaded.

2. **Remove extraneous pictures**. When we first start our blogs, we tend to go out of control with the amount of pictures we add to make our blogs look complete. When I created my blog, I stuffed my sidebar with pictures to make the sidebar more complete. Stuffing my sidebar with pictures made it take longer for my blog to load because loading all of those pictures takes time. It may take a few hundred milliseconds to load each pictures, but those milliseconds add up to seconds, and that load time doesn't include the other factors that slow down your blog. I used to have a big picture of myself on the sidebar

to build brand recognition and a picture of my Twitter Domination training course to get more sales. Taking down those two pictures made my blog load faster, and now instead of promoting the Twitter Domination training course, I promote a free eBook which promotes the Twitter Domination training course.

3. **Make your own pictures**. One of the most common mistakes bloggers make is getting pictures from other websites or Google images and putting those pictures in their blog posts. The problem with putting these pictures on your blog is that they usually take more time to load. If it takes more than a second for one picture on your blog to load, then most of your visitors will abandon your blog before it loads. I made the same mistake as a rookie blogger, and that mistake hurt my blog's speed, and as a result, my search rank. The best pictures for blog speed are small pictures that you create on your own with a tool like Canva. This one tactic made my blog load more than a second faster.

4. **WordPress.org Users—Deactivate the plugins that you are not using**. If your blog is powered by WordPress.org, then you have probably come across several plugins for your blog. Each activated plugin slows your blog down, and although some plugins have a big impact on your blog, other plugins do next to nothing for your blog. Deactivating the plugins you are not using will allow your blog to run faster.

5. **Show a summary of your blog posts instead of the whole text**. The text you put in your blog posts takes time to load, and if your blog posts consist of multiple pictures, then your blog loading time will get longer. You don't want to write shorter blog posts and not

use pictures just because you are worried about your blog's loading time. The solution to this issue is to show a summary of each of your blog posts on the homepage. Instead of showing the entire blog post, you could just show the first paragraph by placing the More tag right after the first paragraph. Only showing one paragraph instead of your entire blog post and repeating that process for all of the blog posts on your homepage will make your blog load faster.

How To Check Your Blog's Speed

The only way to know how much your blog's speed must improve is by knowing your blog's current speed. The web provides a host of tools that let you know your blog's speed, but only one tool matters.

That tool is Google's very own PageSpeed insights. Upon testing your site, Google will give you a grade and offer tips on how to improve. Google gathers the data and gives you feedback within seconds. In the past, other tools dominated this space, but if you want to rank better on Google, use Google's test and follow Google's suggestions. With PageSpeed Insights, Google is literally telling you how to rank better on their search engine.

The Sticky Factor

One factor Google uses to determine how to rank your content is the amount of time your visitors spend engaging with your content. Your content will perform better on search engines if your average visitor spends two minutes engaging with your content compared to if your average visitor spends one minute engaging with your content.

Getting your visitors to stay on your blog for a longer period of time has the SEO advantage, but getting people to stay on your blog boosts the likelihood of your visitors becoming subscribers, and eventually, customers. You want your blog to be sticky and keep visitors on your blog for a long period of time. Here are some ways to make your blog sticky:

1. Make it easy for people to navigate through your blog.
2. Write longer blog posts.
3. Write engaging content.
4. Provide value

I discussed creating valuable, engaging content in Chapter 1, so I will only go into detail about making it easy for people to navigate through your blog and how you can write longer blog posts.

Make It Easy For People To Navigate Through Your Blog

Your visitors have visited numerous blogs before yours (the same applies for YouTube channels, podcasts, and any other form of content). This repeated exposure gave your incoming visitors certain expectations. One of those expectations is easy navigation through the blog's content.

I know that some of my visitors prefer my blog posts about Facebook over my blog posts about Pinterest and vice-versa. It makes sense to allow my visitors access my blog posts about Facebook on one page and my blog posts about Pinterest on another page. How do I do that? The answer is to categorize and tag your blog posts.

Categories and tags make it easier for your visitors to find the exact content they are looking for. If one of my visitors only wants Pinterest related blog posts, then that visitor can go into my Pinterest category. Then, my visitor gets an entire collection of blog posts related to Pinterest. Tags serve the same function.

The difference between a category and a tag is that you must have a small number of categories on your blog so people can find the general content (i.e. blog posts about Facebook, blog posts about Pinterest, etc.), and you can get more specific with tags (i.e. blog posts about Facebook likes, blog posts about getting repins, blog posts about Facebook Groups, etc).

Providing your visitors with a Popular Posts widget (preferably on your blog's sidebar) will also make it easier for visitors to navigate through your blog. The Popular Posts widget allows you to highlight 10 of your blog's most popular blog posts. Those 10 blog posts will then receive more traffic, and visitors will stay on your blog for a longer period of time.

Showing related blog posts at the end of every blog post you write has a similar effect. If one of my visitors finishes reading a blog post about Pinterest, then that visitor most likely wants more Pinterest related content. That is why at the end of my blog posts about Pinterest, I have a related blog posts section which allows me to show previews of three of my Pinterest related blog posts.

Finally, you must have a search box on your blog. Most blog providers like WordPress automatically provide you with a search box, but make sure it is easy for your visitors to find that search box. If you use WordPress, you can go to your blog's sidebar to add a search box or drag your existing one so it's easier to find.

How To Write Longer Blog Posts

Writing longer blog posts is one of the more obvious but overlooked ways to keep visitors on your blog for a longer period of time. The obvious logic behind this tactic is that it takes longer for someone to read a 1,000 word blog post than it takes for someone to read a 500 word blog post. With that said, don't slap words together just to surpass 1,000 words. You want to ensure the value, even when you aim to write longer blog posts.

Longer blog posts tend to keep people on your blog for a longer period of time, but writing longer blog posts has another benefit, an SEO benefit. According to one of the top SEO experts, Neil Patel, most of the top ranked blog posts have over 2,000 words. The most successful blog posts go in-depth and are filled with value.

Continuing to practice every day and writing a longer outline are the two best ways to write longer blog posts like a pro. The amount of effort you put into the preparation determines what you'll get as the final product.

Optimizing Your Content For The Right Keywords

When you publish a piece of content, that content competes with other content for visibility on search engines. Whether it's someone Googling topics in your niche or the YouTube viewer looking for a great video, keywords determine how well your content ranks.

When looking for keywords, don't choose broad topics like "Twitter marketing" where you can find 337 million search results. Instead, look for the long-tail keywords (keyword phrases with more words in them) which have fewer search results. Any niche-related keyword with under 1 million search results displayed is one you should take seriously in one of your pieces of content.

By adding a few words to your original keyword, you'll come out with a less competitive keyword. As of this writing, the phrase "Twitter marketing for beginners" only has 2.63 million results on Google. It's easier to rank for this keyword than for "Twitter marketing." This concept applies to other search engines as well. On YouTube, "Twitter marketing" displays 5.35 million results while "Twitter marketing for beginners" only displays 616,000 results.

Once you discover the right keyword, put that keyword towards the beginning of your content's title. In this case, you can call the content "Twitter Marketing For Beginners" since the keyword works as a standalone title. The keyword doesn't only serve you in the title. For YouTube videos, put the keyword in the first 2-3 lines of the description. For blog posts, incorporate the keyword within the first paragraph. The earlier in your piece you put the keyword, the better.

You can set up the first sentences as something like this:

"Twitter marketing is very advanced, but what about Twitter marketing for beginners?"

This sentence leads into the rest of the content while inserting the keyword towards the beginning of your content. Sprinkling this keyword throughout your content will give it more power. However, overuse will hurt you. If you use the keyword too often, search engines will understand what you're trying to do and rank your content lower.

To hit the sweet spot, I recommend using the SEO Yoast plugin if you run your blog on WordPress.org. If you don't have a blog on WordPress.

org, there is a mathematical way to discover if you're in the sweet spot. Yoast recommends a keyword density between 0.5% and 2.5% (for mathematical purposes, those numbers are 0.005 and 0.025 as decimals).

When you finish writing a description, blog post, or any other written form of content, tally up the word count. Let's say your upcoming blog post is 1,000 words. Here's how you would find the minimum and maximum times you should use the keyword for optimal ranking.

$$1,000 \times 0.5\% = 1,000 \times .005 = 5$$
$$1,000 \times 2.5\% = 1,000 \times .025 = 25$$

In this example, you should aim to use the keyword 5-25 times in your blog post in a non-spammy way. For instance, don't end your blog post like this:

Twitter marketing for beginners
Twitter marketing for beginners
Twitter marketing for beginners (and so on until the 5-25 threshold is obtained)

Instead, think of that first sentence I shared with you. How can you slightly modify sentences in your blog post so they still flow but now display the keyword?

The keyword you choose and how you represent the keyword are critical determinants for where your content ranks. Choosing the keyword before you start writing will allow you to tailor your content towards that keyword. Tailoring your content towards a particular keyword will create more opportunities for you to reference that keyword and thus get your content ranked higher.

PART 2:

CONTENT MARKETING

You can create all of the content you want, but if no one sees that content, you'll be the world's greatest secret. Marketing is a necessary part of the content creator's process because it is the marketing that gives you the ability to create more content.

Let me explain. You create epic content and figure out how to monetize it as we'll discuss in Part 4 of the book. If you market your content, you'll attract more visitors...and more customers. By attracting enough customers, you get to create valuable content full-time. If you don't get the customers, then you won't make the money.

You'll have to juggle your content creation efforts with efforts that lead to revenue (i.e. a job). When you juggle enough things like family, a job, content creation, and many other balls, some are bound to drop.

Igniting your content marketing efforts will make it easier for you to eliminate the tasks and activities that you don't want to actively engage in. We explored outsourcing earlier, but we will now explore how we can make outsourcing and full-time incomes two realities for our content brands instead of beautiful ideas wrapped in theory.

Before you dive deep into the content marketing jungle, you must first get a layout of the land. You must know your plan before you begin to implement. This part of the book will give you the knowledge to grow your content brand with effective content marketing. At the very end of Part 2, we'll discuss how to craft an effective content marketing strategy so you can apply what you learned.

Chapter 7:

BUILDING RELATIONSHIPS

One of the most important things you can do for your content brand is build relationships. As Vin Clancy said during our interview for the Content Marketing Success Summit, "It's such an underrated thing to find other people who can send you traffic, and you can switch it back and forth." If you aren't developing at least one new meaningful relationship every day, your content brand is stagnant at best.

I place an importance on relationships for the following reasons:

- **A lot of people know a lot of things that you don't**. Just because I wrote a book about content marketing doesn't mean I'm the best content marketer on the planet. Some people are better than me, and I want their knowledge. You can also have more overall knowledge than some people, but the 1-2 nuggets of wisdom they know that you don't can make a big difference.

- **Some of these relationships can result in more traffic and sales**. I recruit my own affiliates because that's how important they are for my brand. If they like what you're doing, affiliates will promote your products and landing pages in exchange for commissions based on leads and/or sales.

- **Some relationships lead into other relationships**. As Ray Edwards' Copywriting Academy launch approached, the affiliate manager for Ray's launch contacted me. This affiliate manager's name is Matt McWilliams, and he's the reason I got to connect with Ray. However, that was only the beginning. Without Matt, I would have never interviewed people like Tom Ziglar, Chandler Bolt, Ray himself, and many others. Matt also started up the intro between me and Tom Morkes, and I can say the same exact things about Tom when talking about some of the relationships I've built.

If you're not building relationships, you are missing out on one of the greatest opportunities available. Now you're probably wondering, "Well, that's great…but how do I actually build these relationships?" That's what we'll explore…right now!

The Hack Of All Hacks For Building Relationships

If you look at some of the top influencers' coaching and consultation packages, you'll see a few people who charge hundreds or even thousands of dollars just to get 30 minutes of their time. The most successful people in your niche are extremely protective of their time. Successful people need that mindset to continue growing.

I've taken advantage of many of these coaching and consultation packages to learn from the masters and grow my brand. But here's the important part: I didn't pay a penny.

Why would these influencers give me free access to their coaching and consultation packages, but more importantly, their time? That's because I reframed their packages as guest appearances on my Breakthrough Success

Podcast. This is how you get thousands of dollars' worth of coaching and consultation packages without paying a penny.

For instance, Matt McWilliams charges $2,500 for an hour of coaching. This is something few people can do, but when you run the affiliate launches for people like Ray Edwards, Chandler Bolt, the Ziglar Family, Brian Tracy, Jeff Goins, and many others, you have the ability to charge at that premium.

My one interview with him for the Content Marketing Success Summit lasted a little over an hour. I chose the questions based on the match between what I wanted the answers to and what attendees wanted the answers to. I got a $2,500 service free of charge. That doesn't even include our interview for the Breakthrough Success Podcast.

So far I've framed podcasting as a way to save thousands of dollars (eventually millions if you interview enough people) on coaching and consultation packages. However, during this same timeframe, you and the influencer are bonding. When you have a fun, engaging conversation with someone for an hour, you remember that person, and that person remembers you. When you publish your podcast episode and contact the guest, many times the guest is happy to share the episode with his/her audience.

Virtual summits work in the same way as podcasts, but they are more advanced due to the additional work (recruiting affiliates, setting up the site, creating the funnel, etc.) but well worth the time if you want to pursue that route. We'll explore virtual summits deeper in the Content Monetization part of the book.

Leveraging The Gray Area Of Content To Build Relationships

During our interview for the Content Marketing Success Summit, Andy Crestodina discussed the gray area where certain actions qualify as content creation and content marketing. For each of his blog posts, he'll contact several influencers and get them to collaborate with the blog post.

Not only do you build relationships with influencers, but they also add content to your blog posts. If you write a 1,000 word blog post and get 10 influencers to contribute 200 words each, your blog post is now 3,000 words. Search engines will love you, and you can count on those influencers to share a blog post they were mention in.

After I got some time to unwind from organizing my first virtual summit, I took Andy's advice to heart and started contacting influencers. I was looking for an influencer who could share some advice on the beginning stages of task delegation. I've interviewed Nick Loper twice (one interview for my Breakthrough Success Podcast and the other for my Productivity Virtual Summit), so I knew he'd be very likely to share his insights in one of my blog posts.

When you contact influencers in this manner, understand that they treat their time like gold, so don't give them a big request. Pay attention to how I incorporate the parenthesis.

> Hello Nick,
>
> I am writing a blog post called *How To Play More Offense For Your Business* and one of the tactics I touch upon is delegating tasks. If you are interested, I'd be grateful if you gave some quick advice on how to get started with delegating more tasks (50-100 words but you can do more if you want).

I would feature it in the blog and link back to Side Hustle Nation.

[Closing]

50-100 words is a very small request. Just to give you an idea of how small that order is, the previous sentence and this sentence add up to 31 words. Just one more sentence like this one and Nick is practically done with 50 words. This entire paragraph took me less than a minute to write. Combine that with linking to Side Hustle Nation and this is a low hanging fruit with a tangible upside.

The final part in the parenthesis is "but you can do more if you want." This makes extra content optional, but it doesn't take much time to go from 100 words to 150 words. All of these extra words add more value to the blog post, and I can then tell Nick when the post goes live.

Here was Nick's actual submission which I included in the blog post *How To Play More Offense For Your Business*. The total was 165 words.

> The two main ingredients you need to get started delegating are a log of where you're spending your time and a well-documented process.
>
> The time log will tell you where the biggest opportunities for outsourcing lie. What's sucking up the most of your day? Is that something you HAVE to do, or could someone else reasonably handle it with a little training?
>
> Next, you'll want to have clear process documentation and instructions. This is like your recipe for completing the task, and the more detailed the better. Don't leave anything to chance here, even though you probably take for granted some of the steps,

especially if you've been doing the task yourself for any length of time.

How I normally create the process documentation is I take a screen capture video of myself doing the job and talking through the steps. Then I write out the steps in a Google Doc so I can share both a visual and written version with my assistant.

For this particular blog post, Nick was the only influencer I got on board. However, you can imagine the incremental effect of this strategy by contacting more people. Imagine I got advice from nine additional influencers. Assuming each influencer wrote 165 words, that's an extra 1485 words for your blog post.

That's how the top bloggers constantly write 5,000+ word blog posts that get shared by many influencers.

Be Everywhere To Someone

Podcasting, hosting virtual summits, and collaborating with influencers for your content present incredible opportunities to build relationships with influencers. If there's a particular influencer you want to build a relationship with, be everywhere that influencer will notice you.

If you briefly look at how I use Twitter, you'll notice that I favorite tweets that mention my content and make it a point to respond to as many of my followers as possible. If you want my attention, tweeting @MarcGuberti is a great start. I can't promise replies, but you'll increase your chances of getting on my radar.

I am within the legion of many who interacts with their audiences. Neil Patel makes it a point to reply to every comment, and he gets hundreds of comments within 24 hours for some of his blog posts. Want to get Neil Patel's attention? Comment on each of his newest blog posts. Be everywhere Neil can see you.

For almost any influencer, being everywhere that person looks means the following:

- Like, retweet, and reply to their tweets
- Like, comment, and share their Facebook posts
- Repin their links
- Like, share, and comment on LinkedIn posts
- Comment on their blog posts
- Reply to their email broadcasts
- Engage with them during their Facebook Live broadcasts
- Like and comment on their Instagram pictures
- Mention their handle on your social media accounts when you share their content

By narrowing your focus on an influencer, you'll greatly increase the likelihood of that influencer noticing your presence. Make sure you know the next step for the relationship in advance (are you trying to get the influencer on your podcast, some advice for an upcoming blog post, or something else).

Some people send the email, connect with the influencer on LinkedIn, follow that influencer on his/her social networks and call it a day. Some people get replies right then and there, but that's very rare. Most relationships, especially with the individuals everyone wants to have relationships with, involve much more effort.

I didn't get Seth Godin as a guest on the Breakthrough Success Podcast with a cold email. I created over 150 webpages on Squidoo, the company he and his team created. I created a challenge for other Squidoo users to create more webpages and engage with existing webpages. I saw Seth in person during one of his speeches and got my copy of *Purple Cow* signed. After all of those things and keeping in touch, I then asked him if he'd like to be a guest on the Breakthrough Success Podcast. That's how Episode 16 came to be.

Take this approach with anyone you desperately want to build a relationship with, especially your role models. Keep at it for long enough and your role models will soon be happy to collaborate with you whether that be through a podcast interview, some advice for a book or blog post, or any other way.

The Instant Relationship

One of the many reasons I love hosting virtual summits is because I make several instant relationships. An instant relationship occurs when you have someone you know make an intro.

Before I started the Content Marketing Success Summit, I didn't know who all of the 57 speakers were. I put in the initial effort to get a little over 30 speakers. I then asked each of those 30 speakers if they knew anyone who would be a great fit for the summit. I repeated this process with all of the speakers they referred. I've used this strategy for CMSS and other virtual summits to build dozens of instant relationships.

The foundation of every instant relationship is an individual who both of you know. The common courtesy of instant relationships is to harp about the person who brought the two of you together. Anytime Matt McWilliams connected me with someone, the other person and I usually talk about how great Matt is to break the ice (and if you know Matt, you know he's great at affiliate marketing and launches).

Ask people if they know someone who would be a great podcast guest, virtual summit speaker, person to provide advice for your blog post, or anything else that you are looking for. Other people did the hard work to build the relationships from the ground up, and you can use that to build instant relationships with some of the top players in your niche.

Chapter 8:

REPURPOSING YOUR CONTENT

Chances are people have told you the importance of being omnipresent and utilizing all of the platforms. Doing so is a completely different manner. It takes a lot of time to create a single piece of content, generate revenue, and do everything else for my content brand as is.

This is where content repurposing comes in. The easiest way to be everywhere is to repurpose your content. You can do the work once and put that same piece of work on many platforms with this tactic. Here's an example of what you can do…

1. You create a video and publish it on YouTube, Facebook, and Vimeo
2. You take the video's audio and turn it into a podcast episode
3. You hire someone to transcribe the video and turn it into a blog post
4. You publish the content on your blog, Medium account, and LinkedIn account
5. You hire a graphic designer to turn your blog post into a SlideShare presentation and turn the best quotes from your blog post into pictures that include your branding. You can post these pictures on Pinterest and Instagram.

1 video got published on 10 different platforms in 5 different forms. Assuming all platforms are equal, you did the work once and got 10X the exposure for that same work. It doesn't take much time to upload to Facebook and Vimeo. It doesn't take much time to turn the video into a podcast episode and schedule transcriptions of your videos for your blog and other platforms. You can even outsource these tasks to others, but repurposing your content will make a big difference for your content brand.

Create A Repurposing Schedule

Before you publish your next piece of content, you need to create a repurposing schedule. When you publish a blog post, have a plan to get that blog post on LinkedIn and Medium within the next two weeks. Look for platforms other than LinkedIn and Medium where you can republish your content. Have a plan for turning your podcast episodes into YouTube videos and vice-versa.

You can carry out the repurposing schedule for a piece of content for as long as you desire. The length of your repurposing schedule is the intersection of the number of ways you can repurpose your content and how soon you need to get the content out. Most repurposing schedules range from 2-4 weeks.

Guilt-Free Content Repurposing

For a long time, I felt guilty about repurposing my content. I thought I was pulling a quick one on my audience by providing them with the same exact content they saw before. I felt a little better when I discovered you can slightly modify the content, but it still didn't feel right.

At least, it didn't feel right until I interviewed Jon Nastor for the Content Marketing Success Summit. During our interview, he revealed an important content marketing truth: "No matter how much they love you, [your audience] isn't going to listen to, and read, and watch every single thing you make…use this to your advantage by repurposing your content."

Understanding this truth is the secret to guilt-free content repurposing. Not even your core fans will see everything you post, and I can prove it.

Chances are since you're reading the book to this point, you are either a core fan or gradually developing into a core fan. Let me ask you some questions then. What's the name of the blog post I wrote on July 7, 2017? Which episode did I publish on my Breakthrough Success Podcast on November 30, 2016? When did I publish my first blog post?

To be 100% transparent, if you quizzed me on these same questions, I would have failed. On July 7, 2017, I published the blog post "5 Hacks For Writing Blog Posts Faster." On November 30, 2016, I published the interview with Seth Godin (I might have guessed I published the Seth Godin interview on this day, but it would have been a complete guess). I published the first blog post on marcguberti.com on September 24, 2012.

You might be thinking, "That's a little unfair. These blog posts and the episode were from a while ago."

Fine. What's the name of the blog post I most recently published? Who did I most recently interview for my Breakthrough Success Podcast?

Am I picking on anyone? No. Sometimes I don't even know the answer to these questions because I produce that much content. You can throw these same questions back at me, even when you're talking about some of the people I admire the most. Your core fans will only see a small fraction of your content, so it's your duty to repurpose your content so they can see more of what they missed. If I repurpose "5 Hacks For Writing Blog Posts Faster" in 2018, most of my visitors will see it as a new piece of content.

I've seen content repurposing in books as well. During an audiobook narration, I heard the author read word for word a blog post I previously read on that individual's blog. How did I remember that blog post? Easy. I just happened to read that same exact blog post a few hours ago. If I read that same blog post a month ago, I probably wouldn't have recalled it. Even if I remembered it, the repetition would have been a good refresher.

In a sea of information, you need to resurface the pearls. Search through the depths of your content and find the true winners. Add content to them and re-share them with your audience. Let your old content take on a new form. If you are not doing everything in your power to get your content in front of your targeted audience, you are letting your audience down. They need your content, and you need to get it to them by utilizing various platforms.

The Power Of Multiple Entry Points

Each platform—YouTube, your blog, your podcast, etc.—is an entry point. Providing more entry points puts your visitors into more contact with your content and message. Leveraging as many entry points as possible in an effective manner is the key to building a targeted, highly engaged audience.

Since this strategy has such a potent upside, it's no wonder sports organizations like MLB use it. In case you need a quick reminder, I am the rare breed of New Yorker who is a proud Boston Red Sox fan. Since I live in New York, the Red Sox aren't readily available on television or the radio. I stay up to date on Red Sox games by going on MLB's website to see the pitch by pitch for each game and respond to emails in between innings. My dad (a Yankees fan) uses the MLB At-Bat app to only get updated during score changes because he doesn't watch or listen to games from start to finish.

Let's briefly review some of the platforms MLB uses to communicate with its fans:

1. TV
2. Radio
3. Pitch-By-Pitch for each game on the website
4. Email
5. Social media
6. Live video
7. Apps
8. Blog posts
9. Videos
10. Podcasts
11. Other fans (I'm doing them a favor right now)
12. Text messages

MLB probably communicates with its fans in more ways than what I just mentioned. MLB believes it's important to communicate through a variety of platforms during each game. Sure, MLB has a much bigger budget than you, but embrace this way of thinking now. You might not have the resources to create your own app, but you can definitely start with blog posts, videos, and podcasts. Then you can grow and communicate with your audience through more platforms.

Make it as easy as possible for your audience to consume as much of your content as possible.

Chapter 9:

GUEST APPEARANCES

Before we dive into this chapter, I want to clarify that we'll be tackling guest blogging and being a guest on other people's podcasts as both are guest appearances. With that said, it's time to dive in.

For every content brand, content is the lifeline. The moment you stop producing content is the moment your content brand starts to die. There are some successful bloggers who haven't published blog posts, videos, or podcast episodes in a few months, but they make up for it with virtual summits, training courses, books, and other types of content. Those successful bloggers are the exception to the rule.

Most podcast hosts publish a new episode at least once each week. Most bloggers publish new or repurposed content multiple times each week. Most YouTubers publish one new video every week. Some people depend on outside contributions to fuel their content brands. These are the people you need to contact for more guest appearances.

Get Clear On What You Want*

This is a cliche that I'll expand upon. Getting clear on what you want means just that, getting clear on what you want. Which types of guest blogs and podcasts do you want to appear on? What's the central focus?

However, you have a content brand, so getting clear on what you want takes another meaning. For the top content brands, product and event launches are common place. You don't just want to randomly appear on podcasts and get guest blogging opportunities. You need to think strategically in relation to your launch plans.

One of my goals in the summer leading up to my Productivity Virtual Summit was to get on more podcasts and write more guest posts. However, I couldn't just take any opportunity. I took the opportunities that allowed me to share my insights on productivity. After sharing my insights on productivity, I could more easily provide the plug to my Productivity Virtual Summit. If I had talked about content marketing without mentioning how to host a successful virtual summit, mentioning the Productivity Virtual Summit wouldn't have been as powerful.

For this book, I made it a point to get interviewed on as many podcasts related to content marketing as possible. I temporarily stopped contacting productivity-focused podcasts because my focus changed in relation to the book launch. The next time I launch a product, I'll get on many podcasts and write some guest posts based on that product's topic well in advance.

How To Pitch Your Idea

As I mentioned earlier, content is the lifeline of all content brands. To continue providing their audiences with this important lifeline, content creators that accept guest contributions in the form of guest posts and interviews are looking for people to help them. Believe it or not, they want you. If they like your content, these content creators will publish it as a guest post which gives them more content on their blogs. Some of these same people will interview you for their podcasts. For most podcast hosts, that means 3-4 more interviews to go for this month depending on the first few days of the month (with 30 days in most months, some days of the week repeat five times in a given month. This is why some weekly podcasts must produce five episodes on some months).

With that said, these same individuals have built massive audiences and want to provide them with high value content. They will only accept your guest post submission or your request for an interview if you are the right fit. To make yourself the right fit for any opportunity, you must do some research before beginning the conversation. I promise the research doesn't take much time, but spending 5-10 minutes doing research will make a big difference in your pitch's delivery.

Before submitting a guest post proposal, take a look at other people's guest posts on the blog. These people went through the approval process and ultimately got the "Yes" for publication. For you to get the "Yes," you should mimic these people's style while adding your own flair.

Similarly to guest blogging, take a look at some of the most recent guests who have appeared on a podcast. How can you present in yourself as a similar authority as past guests while adding your own flair? Adding your own flair simply means inserting you into the equation. It isn't something that should receive much thought because it should be easy for you to be yourself.

When conducting this process, look for the guest posts and podcast episodes that have the most engagement. Content brands aren't just in the business of producing more content. They are also in the business of producing engaging content at a faster pace. If you can mention how you will serve this person's audience and connect your pitch with similar topics as the ones that have received high engagement in the past, you're more likely to get the big "Yes."

Get Referred Into More Guest Appearances

Remember how I mentioned a little earlier that, at best, your business is stagnant if you're not building relationships? This is one of the powers that you miss out on if you're not building relationships. At the end of each podcast episode, ask if the person who interviewed you knows of any other podcasts that would be a great fit for you. After writing the guest post, ask if the editor knows any other places that would be a good fit.

Those are commonly discussed tactics in the referred opportunity space, but here's some advice you don't hear very often. Chances are good that I'll be the first one to tell you.

As bloggers and podcast hosts get more influential and they find themselves in a deeper time crunch, they delegate. Many content brand owners delegate their social media activity and continue to delegate as much as possible while staying within the confines of a budget.

Some of them hire middlemen to find guests for their podcasts and contributors for their blogs. Since authority content brands have more money to play with, they'll hire the top talent for finding contributors and/or guests. "Booking agent" at the bottom of an email signature clearly indicates a middleman although not all of them include that in their email signatures. These top tier middlemen are involved with a variety of other podcast or blog owners looking for guests or contributors.

Here's where things get interesting. These middlemen serve their clients by inviting people to contribute content and/or become a guest on the podcast. You don't have to win over the clients. You only have to win over the middleman who serves those clients. If that person likes you, that person will see you as a good fit for his/her clients. Guess who the middleman thinks of first when a new client asks for more guests or contributors? That's right, you!

Finding The Middleman Of Many

In most niche, you can find the right middleman in 5-10 minutes. All you do is search for podcasting and blogging services and see which ones offer to find guests for a host or contributors for a blog owner. Then, it's your job to meaningfully build the relationship with that middleman.

As mentioned before, one of my favorite ways of building relationships is to invite people to be a guest on my podcast. If you do not have this luxury and aren't interested in exploring it right now, you can ask the middleman for a quote, opinion, or insight that you'll feature in your upcoming blog post. People will never turn down free publicity unless they are drowning in it, and most people aren't in that position.

Continue to keep in touch with this middleman, and eventually bring up the fact that you've been a guest on a few podcasts or have written a few guest posts for prominent places. With the preexisting relationship, it's easier to get a middleman to think of you as they hunt for more guests and contributors for their clients.

How To Get Your Content Published Anywhere

If you've thought of guest appearances on various blogs, I'm sure you've thought of writing for some of the biggest brands around. If not, you should definitely start thinking that way.

It's increasingly possible for anyone to get their content published anywhere, whether it's a prominent blog on your niche, *SUCCESS Magazine*, or anywhere else. Each of these places will have different rules. Some blog owners require submissions to be 800 to 1,000 words long while others ask for at least 2,000 words in a given blog post.

Regardless of where you aim to publish your content, here are the steps you need to take:

1. **Look at the guidelines**. The guidelines will reveal the word count, research, and other requirements that will qualify your submission for a meaningful review. Many blogs that accept guest posts make their requirements readily available on a specific page for guest bloggers.

2. **Look around**. Knowing the guidelines is a great start, but there's nothing better than analyzing what already worked. Read the most recently published articles on that blog and write down what they have in common. Pay attention to the introduction, body structure, and conclusion. After determining what works and having the guidelines nearby, you'll be well on your way to getting your content published anywhere.

3. **Come up with the idea**. It's harder to think of a great idea than it is to write a great piece. As you look around, you'll get exposed to great ideas, but you should look to incorporate a blend the old with the new. Let's say you want to write for a social media blog. Most of

the recent blog posts are about Facebook, and while there are some Twitter posts, it's been a while since a new Twitter-related blog post got published. You can then suggest writing an article about Twitter.

4. **Make it trendy**. While this isn't necessary for all blogs, this is a big step if you want to get published on places like *Inc* and *Forbes*. These two content magnates have a constant stream of content flowing through and a library of content already in place. An article pitch containing three ways to get more Twitter followers won't work because places like *Inc* and *Forbes* already have those types of articles. Successful ideas combine key points within a segment of your niche and a trend. For every World Series game, the two best baseball teams of the year go head-to-head. What can each of those teams teach us about social media, content marketing, or your niche? What can a team's rise to the World Series teach us about crafting an effective content strategy? Teaching people while capitalizing on a trend or current event will give your article some extra juice in the search engines and in your chances of getting approved. While this is an advanced tip, it's definitely worth utilizing to give yourself an extra edge.

Chapter 10:

COLLABORATING WITH YOUR AUDIENCE

You can reach out to other individuals for guest appearances, and you can do the same to get guests to contribute to your content brand. However, you don't always have to reach out to people you don't know. Collaborating with your audience will open the floodgates to more content and potential podcast guests than you can ever imagine. The moment you get your audience involved, they really step up to bat for you and do everything they can to hit a home run. Collaborating with your audience builds loyalty, attracts more people, and arms you with legions of contributors and podcast guests.

When I first began to seriously collaborate with my audience, I momentarily wasn't sure about the decision. For a long time, I said that I would be the author of every blog post that ever got published on my blog. This was a big change for me, but the change was necessary. My contributors have provided fresh insights that I couldn't have thought of on my own and have thus made my blog a better place for digital marketers and productivity-focused business owners. I now get to learn new lessons from my own blog which is cool for me.

Qualify Potential Contributors And Guests

For a long time, I didn't accept any guest posts. I wrote the first 1,400 blog posts on my blog, and I intended to keep it that way forever. Then, I saw a need for guest bloggers. Here's how it played out:

#1: I made my blog posts so long and filled up my time to the point where I could only publish 1 blog post per week. This is a big no-no since I'm not publishing enough blog posts.

#2: I have received so many compliments from people who learned from my blog, but I want to learn new things from my blog too. I can't do that if I'm the only person writing the content.

#3: I get to meet new people (the contributors).

#4: Everyone gets more traffic. Let's get started!

Opening the door to guests will save time, but you want to make sure these guests provide you high value content. You don't want any ordinary piece of content to land on your blog. You want top value content—the type content that will turn first-time visitors into returning visitors. You also want content with good SEO.

You don't want to assume that the guest knows your style or how to optimize a blog post for search engines. Guide the guest blogger through the process. When someone comes to you with a good idea, let them know your standards. These are the standards I currently use for aspiring contributors:

- Your guest post must be at least 1,500 words. The more words, the better, but don't sacrifice value (**Why**: longer content is usually more valuable. Search engines know this as they reward lengthy blog posts).
- Link to three of my blog posts (**Why**: linking to my blog posts gives visitors options that keep them on my blog. This requirement keeps

people on my blog longer and lowers bounce rate. The more people stay on my blog, the more likely they are to subscribe and buy my products).

- Include at least three pictures (**Why**: a giant block of text is painful for the eyes to scroll through. Pictures provide good breaks for the eyes, and the human mind registers an image 60,000 times faster than text).

- You have the option to promote one of your blog posts, but not landing pages. You CAN promote your landing pages in your bio (**Why**: WIIFM. In case you don't know what it means, the acronym stands for **W**hat's **I**n **I**t **F**or **M**e).

- All content must be original and not published anywhere else. (**Why:** If the content was published elsewhere and then appears on my blog, that hurts my SEO).

You may include other standards depending on your blog's niche and what exactly you want from contributors. When you allow someone to write a guest post on your blog, that person's content becomes a representation of your content brand.

Make sure you set the standard high so people respect you and your content brand, but don't set the standard impossibly high to the point where most potential guest bloggers look for other options. The challenge is to reach the middle of these two routes.

Get The Ball Rolling With Outside Contributors

Before you contact people within your audience, I recommending contacting people who have written guests posts or appeared on other podcasts in the past. There are several reasons you should implement this approach:

1. No matter how large your audience is, there are more people not in your audience than there are people in your audience. Even Facebook with 2 billion users doesn't have half of the 7 billion population.
2. You get to build relationships which are critical to success.
3. You get into the habit of reaching out which can reliably provide you with consistent content and guests over time.
4. Your audience starts to take note that you accept contributors and guests. Some people in your audience will start asking you if they can contribute or be a guest.
5. You attract a new audience of people who are looking for opportunities like this.

Once you get the outside contributors and guests on board, it's time to communicate with your audience.

Building Momentum With The Help Of Your Audience

When I'm planning a big event, I always ask my audience to get involved in some way. For the Content Marketing Success Summit, I emailed me entire list inviting my subscribers to pitch themselves as potential speakers for the summit. I got seven speakers directly from that one email and a few more speakers if you include referrals.

You can ask people to submit their guest post topic ideas and/or why they would be a great fit for your podcast. If you have a decent sized audience, you can expect to get a few responses by the end of the day. You will then collaborate with these people in your audience to create content, and at the end of the collaboration, interview or guest post, ask them to refer other people you can collaborate with. By continuing this cycle and growing your content brand in the process, you'll have an endless stream of guests for your podcast and/or contributors for your blog.

The Different Collaboration Relationships

For some of your content, it is better to do most of the content creation and have many people do different fractions of the work. For other relationships, the contributor will do the bulk of the work.

So far we have focused on the relationship in which the person you find does most of the work. The guest blogger writes the entire guest post that you then look over and the guest for your podcast shows up with his/her expertise.

The other collaboration relationship puts the bulk of the work on you. In this relationship, you contact many people and ask for a quick opinion, recommendation, or advice. The idea is to gather as many expert opinions as possible in what are called Expert Round-Up posts. These posts are great for relationships and visibility because many of the people you feature in the round-up tend to share your post with their audiences when it gets published.

For instance, I wrote a blog post called "22 Experts Recommend Their Favorite Blogging Tools." With the help of the 22 experts, this blog post quickly became a 4,000+ word behemoth, and with many of those same experts sharing the blog post with their audiences, it became one of the most popular pieces on my blog.

How To Make The Outreach A Little Easier

I'm sure some people are thinking about the work involved with getting 22 experts to recommend their favorite blogging tools. The truth is it takes a fair amount of work, but not in the ways most people would expect.

Getting the 22 experts to share their insights was actually the easy part. I used HARO (Help A Reporter Out) to get most of the experts. HARO is one of the most popular free PR-generating services around. You can contact people one by one and get a bunch of great insights, recommendations, quotes, and opinions. Leveraging HARO allowed me to get those 22 experts to share their favorite blogging tools in a shorter period of time.

Then it was a matter of reading through everyone's applications. I read…and read…and read. I said no to some people and added other people's contributions to the ever growing blog post. Reading everyone's contributions took far more time than contacting everyone, but that was largely because I used HARO to find the experts.

The most time consuming part of the process was keeping in touch with everyone and asking them to share the blog post when it went live. Of course, this task was also the most rewarding as you'll get a wave of traffic heading your way. As your content brand grows, you can eventually delegate this part of the process or delegate the entire process depending on how you feel about the work involved with creating an Expert Round-Up post.

Chapter 11:

GROWING YOUR EMAIL LIST

Your email list is your brand's most important digital asset. If your favorite social network goes through an algorithm change, or someone in charge decides to increase the pay-to-play atmosphere, you have lost your ability to communicate with many people in your audience.

When you get your social media followers and visitors onto your email list, you own that traffic. You can tell these people about your latest content and get these people to return to engage with your content again and again. The email list also outclasses social media and every other platform as the highest ROI generator.

For many people, this isn't new knowledge. We know the email list is important, and it seems like every top content creator's biggest regret was not starting an email list sooner. However, many business owners have small email lists and want to do everything in their power to grow their email list. Even the people with hundreds of thousands of email subscribers want more.

In a sea of email list growth tactics that seems to grow as the days go by, it's hard to anchor down and choose which tactics you'll utilize. This chapter will provide a variety of tactics that will help you grow your email list. Some will be more impactful than others.

At the end of this chapter, I want you to choose one tactic and implement it because if you don't implement anything from this chapter, growing your email list will still feel overwhelming. Growing your email list will feel overwhelming in the beginning because there's so many ways to do it, and the presence of many options can paralyze our decision making. The result is a bunch of tactics that work but forever stay in the junk draw. These tactics work, but you need to implement at least one of these tactics right away so you can add more tactics to your arsenal.

50 Tactics To Grow Your Email List

The digital landscape is always changing right in front of us. More opportunities for growing an email list get presented as the days go by. Live streaming was recently introduced to us a little over a year ago.

Based on the number of articles and videos about live streaming since its existence, it seems as if live streaming apps like Periscope have been around for decades.

It is getting harder and harder for us to imagine life without this changing digital landscape.

No matter how often the digital landscape changes, the story will remain the same. Your email list is your most valuable asset. It's where the money and ultimate engagement reside.

To grow an email list, you either increase the conversion rate or you get more traffic that gets directed to an opportunity to join your list. Those are the two underlying principles behind all 50 of these tactics.

#1: Create A Bunch Of Landing Pages

HubSpot came out with an article that helped us learn the importance of creating landing pages in bulk. More landing pages means more free offers that people can choose between…and therefore a bigger email list.

If you have Offer A and Offer B, some people won't like Offer A, but they'll love Offer B and vice-versa. Now imagine having 40 offers. Your visitor could be non-responsive to 39 of your offers, but as long as the visitor responds to at least one offer, you got another qualified lead on your email list. Why 40 landing pages? That's how many HubSpot says will help you get more leads.

#2: Put A Site Wide Pop-Up On Your Blog

Pop-ups…you either love them or you hate them. Regardless of how you feel about pop-ups, they absolutely work for your email list.

The more your pop-up offer matches your blog's content, the more subscribers you will get. If people aren't interested in the pop-up offer, they can simply x out of the pop-up and continue reading the blog post.

#3: Create Udemy Courses

Udemy is a one of those unexpected places for building an email list since it is more known for course building. You can send email blasts to the students enrolled into your courses. You can segment them based on their progress through your course, when they enrolled, and which courses they are enrolled in.

The key to using Udemy to grow your email list is to promote free coupon codes of your courses into Facebook group pages that are specifically for free Udemy coupons. I got over 60,000 students by leveraging this strategy who I can send emails to.

Sending emails to over 60,000 Udemy students is free, but there are some catches. You can only promote your Udemy courses or learning material that students can access without entering personal info (i.e. an email address), and you can only send four educational and two promotional emails per month to students of a given course.

However, you can send these students to your blog posts and YouTube videos with a CTA at the end. Sending Udemy students to a blog that displays a pop-up is fine too.

#4: Put Your Udemy Courses On SkillShare

If you put your course on Udemy, you might as well put it on SkillShare. You'll get access to more students who you can email and you'll also make more revenue.

If you don't feel like uploading Udemy videos into SkillShare, then hire a freelancer to get the job done. Putting your Udemy courses on SkillShare allows you to get more out of the same work.

#5: Use HelloBar To Promote Your Landing Page

HelloBar is a plugin that allows you to put a message at the top of your blog. Within this message, you can tell people about your landing page offer. Then you get to add a button which links to your landing page.

Since HelloBar rose to fame for putting that message at the very top of a blog, the plugin has added the capability of putting your message on the bottom left, bottom right, top left, or top right for your blog. I choose to display another offer on the bottom right of my blog.

#6: Leverage Your Blog's Sidebar

The goal of a blog sidebar is to grab attention while presenting a compelling offer. The sidebar won't be the highest converting part of your blog, but people will remember your offers.

To get more conversions from your sidebar, fill your sidebar up with awesome pictures that feel like a part of the blog post. Better yet, have different sidebars for different content categories.

When reading Kim Garst's blog post about Facebook live streaming, she offers her free eBook 27 Killer Facebook Post Ideas 2.0 on the sidebar. For her blog post about tweeting during live events, she offers her free eBook on Twitter hashtags on the sidebar.

These two free offers promoted on the sidebar are relevant to the blog post. The free offers almost feel like a part of the blog post itself.

#7: Use UpViral To Create A Landing Page

UpViral is a great tool for creating landing pages in a few minutes. They are basic which can sometimes help out with getting conversions.

The magic happens when someone subscribes. They immediately get sent over to a Thank You Page that incentivizes visitors to share the landing page URL.

For my Thank You Page, I encourage people to get more leads. Each person who brings in five leads gets exclusive videos.

With this set-up, people now have an incentive to drive more leads to my landing page. The final result is that the people who get access to the three exclusive videos add five people to my email list.

UpViral can identify fraudulent sign-ups so you don't have to worry about people gaming the system just to get the exclusive videos or content that you offer.

#8: Promote Your Landing Pages On Social Media…A Lot

You can't complete any list like this without saying "promote on social media." Use Facebook, Twitter, Pinterest, and all of the other social networks that you can think of.

However, don't just stop at promoting your landing page once in a given day. At least 25% of my social media posts send people over to one of my landing pages.

Most of your social media audience will not see your first post about your landing page. The more times you promote your landing page on social media, the more traffic those landing pages will get from your social media efforts.

#9: Include A CTA In All Of Your YouTube Videos

It's easy to promote a landing page on most social networks. Write the right copy, include the link, and then post it.

YouTube is completely different. While the description is a great place to promote your landing page similarly to how you would on other social networks, YouTube requires an in-video call-to-action.

At the end of my YouTube videos, I utilize a call-to-action. It leads people to my free eBook 27 Ways To Get More Retweets On Twitter. As you create more landing pages, you can also promote specific landing pages that are relevant to the video topic. People who make it to the end of your video appreciate the value you provided. That's the exact moment you want to provide those viewers with the CTA.

#10: Appear On Other People's YouTube Channels

Some YouTube channels allow guest contributions similar to guest posts. While these channels are hard to find, it is possible to do a guest video on someone else's channel where you provide the CTA. Tim Schmoyer of Video Creators provides this opportunity for people with YouTube tips to share. Opportunities like this are hard to find but are well worth it for your growth.

#11: Create A Podcast With A CTA

I can't say enough good things about podcasts. Podcasting allows you to share your expertise in the form of audio. In a world fueled by content and video creation, audio is one of the lesser utilized methods of getting traffic. If you utilize it well, podcasting can bring in a massive amount of traffic. At the beginning and end of your podcast episodes, you can introduce several CTAs such as leaving a review and subscribing to the podcast.

The critical CTA to mention within all of your podcast episodes is a free offer relevant to that particular episode. When you mention the free offer, make sure the link is easy for people to remember. This is important because podcasts are all audio unless your listeners are also reading through the show notes.

When Mike Stelzner asks for a review on iTunes, he refers to the link as socialmediaexaminer.com/itunes. He does not refer to the link as https://itunes.apple.com/us/podcast/social-media-marketing-podcast/id549899114?mt=2&ls=1

Both lead to the same destination, but the first one is much easier to remember. Please have mercy on the person who must recite the longer link. While this is an example that relates to podcast reviews, the same general rule also applies to landing pages.

#12: Write Guest Posts With The Optimized Author Bio

Writing guest posts on relevant blogs is a great way to get more traffic from people reading your guest posts, and you'll get a high-value backlink. Whenever you write a guest post, you'll usually get a quick bio of yourself. Within 1-2 sentences, you need to let readers know where else they can find you on the web. Within this quick bio, you can direct people over to your landing page. In my Business2Community bio, I provide the CTA to check out my landing page.

"Marc Guberti is a 19 year old digital marketing expert, blogger, and author. If you want to get more retweets and spread your message farther using Twitter, you can grab Marc's free eBook, 27 Ways To Get More Retweets On Twitter."

My name links to my blog and the eBook's name links to the landing page.

#13: Promote Your Landing Page During Podcast Interviews

The way almost all podcast interviews work is that after all of the questions have been answered, the guest has the ability to tell listeners where they can find the guest on the web.

When you are a guest on a podcast episode, mention your landing page. When I first started getting on more podcasts, I had bullet-points in front of me specifically for that question so I know what to say when I have to promote my landing page. Now I no longer need those bullet points thanks to constant practice.

#14: Provide Perks

Give your subscribers certain perks (i.e. discounts and exclusive content) that people outside of your email list won't get. Then, make it known to your blog visitors that only subscribers get these perks. These perks will incentivize more of your visitors to subscribe.

#15: Design Matters

The way you present your free offer is just as important as the value of that free offer. If your free offer has a bad design, people won't want to enter their email addresses.

One reality of life is that we all judge a book by its cover. Let's say you have two identical books with different book covers. It doesn't matter that the content for both of them is the same. The better looking cover will capture more subscribers for your email list. The better the design, the better the perceived value of your free offer. Once you get people in, all you have to do at that point is deliver on your subscribers' expectations (better yet, go above and beyond).

#16: Live Stream Your Message

Live streaming is the hot thing right now. I think it will stay hot for a very long time (if it ever cools down at all). The attractive lure to live streaming is that you get immediate results. Promote a landing page with an easy to remember URL, and you'll instantly get a bunch of subscribers if you have a large enough live audience.

On Periscope, you either need the easy to remember URL or a link to your landing page within your bio. For Facebook Live however, you can drop a link straight into the comments section. If you feel too stressed to include those links during your live stream, hire a freelancer who will get the job done.

#17: Co-Create An Offer

I have created over 20 courses on Udemy. I created some of those courses alone while I created other courses with some help.

The courses I have co-created with other instructors have combined to bring in more students which I can communicate with at any time. If I didn't co-create some of my courses, I would have lost out on tens of thousands of extra students.

Co-creation is not something that only exists within Udemy. You can co-create a free offer with someone else and share the subscribers who sign-up for the co-created free offer.

The cool part about this type of co-creation is that both you and the person who helped you create the free offer will be actively promoting the landing page. You'll be helping each other out.

#18: Create A Product With An Affiliate/JV Program

This is an advanced method to grow your email list, but depending on who promotes your offers, you can get tens of thousands of new subscribers overnight.

To get at that level, you need a top-notch product and many connections. But even if you don't expect to get 10,000 subscribers in one day, you could still get hundreds or thousands of subscribers that you wouldn't have gotten on your own.

At any moment you get, leverage other people's marketing for the growth of your content brand. Your landing page will reach more people and you'll be putting in the same amount of work you put in now.

#19: Publish A Kindle Book

When promoted correctly, a Kindle book can bring in a massive amount of email subscribers. Within all of your Kindle books, promote a free offer relevant to the book people are reading.

Promoting your free offer on the first page is important because anyone can see that offer through Amazon's free preview option, even if they don't buy your book. Readers will feel like they're getting a steal by joining your email list. Just like that, you'll have plenty of new subscribers coming your way.

#20: Put Your Presentations Up On SlideShare

SlideShare is a social network that people either seem to not use at all or use often. It takes time to create a quality SlideShare presentation while it only takes a few seconds to send out a quality tweet.

However, SlideShare presentations have viral potential if you make yours awesome and promote it to enough people. Self-published author Steve Scott uses SlideShare to grow his email list. For one of his Traffic and Income report, Steve mentioned that he got 1,915 new subscribers from SlideShare within three months. That's an average of 638 new subscribers per month just from SlideShare. Steve did hire a freelancer to help out with the presentations to save time, but it will be worth the money if you can get those new subscribers to buy some of your products.

#21: Interact With Your Audience

Interacting with your audience allows you to build trust. The people you interact with will be more likely to enter their email address when your free offer comes up.

Even if you only interact with your audience for five minutes each day, you are creating more trust. The trust results in more people promoting your content and subscribing for updates.

The more interactive your content brand is, the more your audience will love you. If you want to take this level of interaction to the next level, you can create a podcast in which you answer your audience's questions.

#22: Analyze Your Results

If you create landing pages, get subscribers, but then don't analyze the results, you are probably missing out on a huge opportunity. Analyzing the results allows you to discover which of your landing pages have the best conversion rates and which ones you are promoting the most.

Let's say you have two landing pages. Landing Page A has an 80% conversion rate. It's the king of all landing pages. Landing Page B has a 5% conversion rate which puts it at rock bottom.

You promote them equally and they each get 100 daily visitors. The mistake lies right there. You are promoting them equally. If you have a landing page with an 80% conversion rate, you need to promote that landing page far more often than any of your other landing pages. If one of my landing pages had a 5% conversion rate, I would stop promoting it or completely change that landing page and see if that made a difference (normally I suggest testing out one new change at a time over 1-2 weeks, but for a landing page with a 5% conversion rate that just asks for a name and email address, it's worth a complete overhaul).

#23: Offer A Content Upgrade

A content upgrade is exclusive content or video content that is related to the blog post your visitor finished reading. The only way to get access to the content upgrade is to enter an email address.

Content upgrades are valuable because they are specific offers based on the specific content your visitors were reading. While content upgrades create extra work, utilizing them right can give you a big boost in subscribers. I only recommend using content upgrades for your most popular pieces of content to maximize the results you get from your time.

#24: Sprinkle Relevant CTAs To Landing Pages Throughout Your Blog Posts

When you have a content upgrade available, you want to reference it at the beginning and the end of your blog posts. That way, your visitors are constantly reminded of your content upgrade. If you don't utilize content upgrades, then promote a free offer relevant to the content your visitor is reading. If someone is reading an article about cooking the best chocolate cake, you can promote a free eBook on how to cook your five favorite chocolate cakes at the beginning and end of your content.

#25: Write An Expert Round-Up Article

Writing Expert Round-Ups makes a return because this idea is rarely utilized and yet so powerful. These articles get plenty of traffic because people love sharing articles that they get featured in.

You ask several experts for their #1 tip in something. You choose the best tips and put them in your expert round-up article. Then you email the experts and let them know when the article gets published. Ask them to promote it if they are interested (make it their choice to promote instead of sending out a pushy request).

This strategy works for getting traffic, and more traffic in most cases equates to more subscribers. To ensure you get more subscribers, include a relevant content upgrade within the expert round-up article.

#26: Optimize Your Current Traffic

Let's say you get 100 daily visitors on your blog and you get five of them to subscribe each day. What if you made a few changes on your blog to get 10 daily subscribers with that same audience.

In a rush to grow and get more exposure, some bloggers make the mistake of forgetting to optimize the experience for the audiences they have already built.

#27: Advertise Your Landing Page

Facebook ads, AdWords, YouTube ads, and any other type of online ad can be used to promote your landing page. With that said, you should only begin to advertise your landing page once it is proven to make money. You should know how much money you make per subscriber so you can identify what a conversion is worth to you.

For instance, if each subscriber is worth an average of $2, and your Facebook ad gets you new conversions at a rate of $3 per subscriber, you need to stop that Facebook ad or make your average subscriber worth more than $3. There are plenty of advertising options, but understanding this principle will allow you to determine if you are making a good investment or not.

#28: Use Permission Marketing On Reddit

The Reddit community is fierce if you get on their wrong side, but if you get on their right side, you'll get a lot of added exposure. The key to Reddit is leveraging permission marketing. The Reddit community will come at you full force (don't underestimate the Reddit community) if they think you are self-promoting. If you ask for permission, you have a chance at going viral.

#29: Capitalize On The 404 Error Redirect

When people enter the wrong URL, they get sent over to the 404 error page. Some 404 error pages don't bring people back to the blog. Others simply reference the homepage. Why not reference your free offer. Your 404 error page can have a message like this:

"Sorry! What you were looking for does not exist, but I don't want to leave you empty-handed…"

Then you promote your free offer, and BOOM! People who were once lost are now sent over to your landing page.

#30: Keep Your Current Subscribers On Your List

If you get 100 subscribers per day but you lose 100 subscribers per day, then you are not growing. Part of growing your email list is providing an awesome experience for your current subscribers so they are more likely to stick around.

#31: Host A Free Giveaway

Giveaways are great for getting subscribers because few people would turn away the opportunity to get something just by entering an email address. When these people subscribe, you present them with a free offer that everyone gets. Maybe it's a report or a video series. Regardless of what you choose, everyone gets it.

Only a few people will actually win your giveaway. Using UpViral to reward points to the people who share your giveaway landing page will result in more people participating.

But you want the right people to participate. Don't be the marketer who offers a $50 Amazon Gift Card. EVERYONE wants that. You'll get a lot of subscribers, but most of them won't be qualified. You will have to pay extra for having those subscribers on your list, and you'll see a big drop when you announce the Amazon Gift Card winner.

To avoid that heartache, offer a giveaway that only the people in your niche would care about. Matt McWilliams hosted one of the best free giveaways for getting targeted subscribers. He didn't offer an Amazon Gift Card. He offered five free books all related to his niche. People interested in reading those books participated in the giveaway by entering their email addresses and promoting the giveaway on their social networks for extra points. People not interested in the books didn't sign-up. Most if not all of the leads he got from that giveaway were targeted leads.

#32: Add A Link To Your Landing Page In Your Email Signature

Email is one of the top forms of communication today. Including your landing page link within your email signature can give it more exposure. The impact of this method is dependent on how many emails you send in a given day. The more emails you send each day, the more subscribers you'll get from this method. With that said, avoid getting trapped in your inbox. This is more of a set-and-forget bonus that you shouldn't rely on for the bulk of your email list's growth.

#33: Promotion Exchanges

The word exchange has a bad rap in the online world. Most of us are introduced to the word "exchange" in the online marketing sense when people either ask for link exchanges even though their niches are completely different or following a random, non-targeted person just for the follow back.

Promotion exchanges can put your landing page in front of a massive audience if you know how to utilize exchanges. It is ideal to do a promotion exchange with someone who has a similar audience size as you. There are several promotion exchanges you can use:

- Promote each other on your social networks.
- Send email blasts to your lists promoting the other person's landing page.
- Interview each other on your podcasts (if you both have podcasts).

The opportunities are endless, but the second option works for growing your email list. By promoting someone else's landing page to your email list, your landing page also gets more exposure. The final result is both of your email lists will grow. Imagine how much bigger your email list would be if you did this with dozens of people.

#34: Collect Email Addresses At Events

The old-fashioned methods still work. Go to the event with a notepad, pen, and paper. On the piece of people, provide a section where people enter their email address. Let people know on that piece of paper and through your conversation about the free offer these people will get upon writing down an email address. You can segment all of these people on a custom list where you thank them for meeting you at the event to develop a more personalized relationship.

#35: Host A Webinar

Webinars convert very well because they provide free value and are time sensitive. If you have a monthly webinar, your audience will begin to expect webinars. While you'll see plenty of people from your email list attend your webinar, you'll also attract new subscribers into the mix.

#36: Host A Webinar With A Guest

Hosting a webinar with a guest is better than hosting a webinar on your own because the guest will do some of the promotion. Some of the people on your guest's email list will subscribe to the webinar. If you go this route, I suggest having, at the minimum, a monthly webinar with an influential guest so you provide value to your audience, and your guest's efforts allow you to expand your audience as well.

#37: Utilize Social Proof

Not everyone can leverage social proof equally, but leverage it whenever you can. Buffer utilizes powerful social proof in one of their opt-in boxes which read at the time of writing "Join 42,023 good-looking folks who get our latest content first :)"

Within this opt-in box, Buffer indicates that 42,023 people are on their email list. This social proof indicates Buffer is a popular blog, and people perceive popular blogs with valuable content. Buffer is no exception to the rule. If you haven't checked out their blog yet, I recommend giving it a look. The value the Buffer team provides within every blog post is amazing!

#38: Write Longer Content

Longer content increases the reader's time on your blog. In addition, the longer your blog post is, the higher you'll rank on search engines. More visibility results in a bigger email list, and if you can get first-time visitors to stay on your blog for 10 minutes, they will definitely want to stay updated.

#39: Include The Landing Page Link In Your Social Media Bios

This is an easy change you can make to get more subscribers. Most people link to their blog home pages within their social media bios. Unless your home page is a beautiful landing page, that URL needs to be changed. On my Twitter bio, I am always promoting a specific landing page as my link instead of my blog's homepage.

#40: Make It Easier For People To Share Your Blog's Content

I use the Click To Tweet plugin by CoSchedule to make it easier for people to tweet my content. It allows me to craft a prewritten tweet, and when people click on the prewritten tweet, they then get the option to tweet it to their audiences.

I know that not everyone will tweet my content with that plugin. However, some people will, and that creates more exposure. Don't just stop with the social sharing buttons on the top or bottom of your blog posts. Include chances throughout your content for people to share it with their audiences.

#41: Pay With A Post

I have not used this method myself, but from what I've heard, it's powerful. The way pay with a post works is that visitors can only read some of your blog post. The rest are blocked. The only way people can get access to the rest of the blog post is by sharing that blog post on one of their social media accounts.

That's how you get the name: Pay With A Post.

The website I recommend based on my research (but not implementation) is Pay With A Tweet. Pay With A Tweet has expanded to include other posting options in addition to tweeting.

#42: Build Relationships With Influencers

Building relationships with influencers helps out in the long-term. If you create a product with a joint venture program, you will know several influencers in advance who would be happy to help you out.

As mentioned before, you can also host webinars with influencers as guests, and some of them may promote your content a few times each week on their social media accounts. Having a relationship with an influencer gives you the potential to spread your message to the people within that influencer's audience. Some influencers will help you more than others, but any extra visitor you can get should be highly appreciated.

#43: Include An Opt-In Box At Your Blog's Footer

Ever scroll to the bottom of a blog post? Maybe you wanted to go to the next page and see the next batch of blog posts, but you scrolled down too quickly. Maybe you were looking for the blogger's contact me page.

Some people make it to the blog's footer, and within that footer, you can include an opt-in box. The Buffer Blog's opt-in box which I mentioned earlier is at the footer of their blog.

Some of the people who make it to your blog's footer engage with a ton of your content to get there. These people will be more likely to subscribe since they engaged with your content for a long period of time.

#44: Improve Your Homepage

The homepage is one of the most visited pages on your blog. Most homepages lead to a bunch of blog posts. While this is a great way to get more blog readers in the short-term, it's a disaster for the long-term.

Your homepage needs to make your blog easy to navigate while promoting a can't miss CTA. On Pat Flynn's homepage, the CTA is to click the "Start Here" button. Scrolling down will reveal more CTAs on his homepage. Seth Godin took a simplistic approach with his homepage. There are several CTAs, and if you have been reading Seth's content long enough, you'll probably click on all of those CTAs.

Both of these homepages include CTAs and easy navigation throughout the blog. Some subscribe buttons work better at the top while others work better at the bottom. You need to test the button placements to determine what works for your homepage, but you must make it as easy as possible for your visitors to subscribe.

#45: Create Urgency Around Some Of Your Offers

If you have enough landing page, test creating offers that are time sensitive. Webinars are a great example of this. People know the webinar will be packed with value and that it won't be up forever. Do that with one of your free offers.

You won't get consistent growth, but you'll get a spike of growth from that one landing page. Your other landing pages can bring in the consistent growth.

#46: Republish Your Content Elsewhere

Content creators make it a standard practice to repurpose as much of their content in as many ways as possible. Republishing your blog posts on other places like Medium and LinkedIn is one of those ways. Including your landing page link within the byline will help you get more subscribers directly from your republished content.

As your republished blog posts appear on more blogs, people will remember you. Some of them may decide to search for you on Google or social media and come to your blog.

Provide these people with an enticing offer and BOOM, you have more subscribers.

#47: Make The Free Offer Better Than Anything Else Out There

I believe this is an underrated tip that can be better understood with a comparison to blog posts. There are billions of blog posts, and chances are millions of those blog posts are about growing your email list.

To make one of your blog posts stand out from the crowd, go all-in and spend hours of your time on that one blog post. The same goes for any other type of content. Are you spending hours of your time crafting your free offer? Are you truly going all-in?

There are some blog posts that outclass most of the free offers someone with an email address could get access to. Create free offers that would outclass any blog post imaginable. Combine that with excellent design, and you'll have an offer that people won't be able to resist.

#48: Create An Infographic With Your Landing Page Link

Infographics have the potential to go viral. This is old news, but how you set up the infographic determines the success you get out of it. One strategy you can use with your infographic is to include the link to your landing page at the bottom of the infographic. Most people just include the link to their blog homepage, but the link to your landing page (or a homepage that functions similarly to a landing page) will have a bigger impact on your email list growth.

#49: Waiting List For Your Upcoming Product

More people than ever are launching their products and achieving massive success. Depending on the people in your joint venture program combined with your own efforts, it's possible to make seven figures in a few weeks.

But what happens after the launch? What happens to the people who missed out and didn't hear anything about the launch? After the launch, any pages related to the launch become redirect links. The redirect links lead to a landing page that encourages people to subscribe so they can be notified when the product is available again. There's also a free offer included to increase the desire someone would have to provide his/her email address.

#50: Make Your Landing Page Load Faster

If the landing page takes 30 seconds to load, are you sticking around? Probably not, and a landing page that's one second slower is bound to get fewer conversions. Patience is a virtue, but almost none of us have it. In certain scenarios, we want to achieve or get access to something immediately. To Amazon, site speed time is critical. According to an article from Fast Company, Amazon loses $1.6 billion in sales each year if the site loads one second slower. Google said that if their site loaded 0.4 seconds slower, they would lose over 8 million searches per day and plenty of ad revenue. You won't suffer that type of loss if your landing page is one second slower, but you'll definitely get fewer conversions.

Prepare Your Landing Page For Success

When someone visits your blog, they may see your pop-up within a few seconds depending on how you set that up in the dashboard. If a visitor reads your entire blog post, that visitor should see the opt-in form. However, not all of your visitors will see your landing page. This isn't good since leading people to your landing page is one of the best way to get subscribers.

How come? The answer is that a landing page offers a free incentive and asks for an email address. While a pop-up can be evaded by clicking the "x" in the corner and a opt-in form at the bottom of a blog post can be looked over, a simple but clear landing page grabs a visitor's attention for a longer period of time since there is no "x" button.

Although not everyone who visits my landing page actually enters an email address, I get more subscribers from my landing pages than anywhere else on my blog. While a blog has a sidebar, menu, and blog posts (just to name a few of the distractions), a landing page contains zero distractions.

Now that you know why your landing page is the most important page on your blog, the next step is to know how to optimize your landing page for success.

My landing page for 27 Ways To Get More Retweets On Twitter has two opt-in boxes. The opt-in box on the top gets the most attention because it is right next to my free eBook. If a visitor scrolls down to learn more about the eBook, then the second opt-in box is waiting.

Below the picture of the eBook is a list of benefits associated with the eBook with green checkmarks next to each benefit. You want to inform your visitors how they will benefit from your free offer so they have a better reason to enter their email addresses.

Many landing pages also come with short descriptions. I have seen all kinds of descriptions for numerous landing pages. The best descriptions explain why your free offer is a must-have. For my landing page, I explained why getting your content to spread on the web is more important than ever.

I then connect that to tweets and highlight my eBook as the solution—you get to learn how to get more retweets, and getting more retweets will allow your content to spread farther.

At this point, getting the color of the text right is one of the two final touches. Final touches are easy to overlook, but that doesn't mean they are insignificant. Choose colors for your text that match the text of your free offer (I use light blue for the text "27 Ways To Get More Retweets On Twitter" and "How to make your tweets reach out to more people" to match the eBook cover). My favorite color to use is the color blue because it builds trust between your visitors and your brand. No wonder Facebook, Twitter, PayPal, Skype, WordPress, Samsung, HP, Dell, Ford, American Express, and NASA (just to name a few) have blue colored logos. Each color has its own meaning. Test different colors for your text and see which color combo allows you to get the most subscribers.

- Blue: Loyalty, wisdom, strength, trust, and calmness
- Red: energy; creates urgency (no wonder this color is often used in clearance sales)
- Green: associated with the wealthy, used to relax people in stores
- Yellow: optimistic and youthful; attention-grabber
- Orange: aggressive; creates a call-to-action
- Pink: romantic and used to market products to women and girls
- Black: powerful and sleek; used to market luxury products
- Purple: used to soothe and calm

The second overlooked final touch is the terminology you use for your opt-in button. When a visitor clicks the button, it may say "Download Now," "Subscribe Now," or something similar. Here are some tips:

1. NEVER use the word "submit." HubSpot wrote a brilliant article about landing pages which explained that using submit in the button will hurt your landing page's ability to get more subscribers.

2. Test out different text. Download Now, Get FREE Access, Get Your Free eBook, and Subscribe For Updates are four expressions you can put in your landing page's button to get more subscribers.

These two overlooked final touches both impact how many subscribers you get from your landing page. You should create multiple landing pages, promote them all, and see which landing pages convert the most. You can learn from the most and least successful landing pages. Continue implementing what works and stop implementing what doesn't work.

Chapter 12:

CREATING AN EFFECTIVE CONTENT MARKETING STRATEGY

Now that you are armed with content marketing tactics you can use to level up your game, it's time to create a strategy that puts some of those tactics into motion. I say some instead of all because you want to start out with a simple strategy and then expand on it as the implementation becomes easier and you can assess your results. Once you find your groove, focus on mastering one tactic at a time instead of being mediocre at all of them.

For any strategy to work, you must have a definite aim and a mapped out path to achieve your desired results. By the time you reach your destination, you'll realize that the actual path you take will be different from the one you mapped out. However, mapping out a path will help you reach the destination sooner even if you feel off-course at times. This is similar to how airplanes are off course for the majority of the flight and the pilot's role is to continually get the airplane back on track so it reaches the correct destination.

Once we have a definite aim and a mapped out path, we can then go deeper into how we'll implement this strategy.

Have A Definite Aim

A definite aim is a measurable goal that is in between what you deem as challenging and what you deem as impossible. This "in-between zone" will help you crack out of your comfort zone, and only by doing this will you realize that the impossible was possible all along. For instance, you may believe 100,000 monthly visitors isn't possible for you right now, but what about an extra 1,000 visitors this month? Little by little, you can move yourself towards and past seemingly impossible goals.

An important part of the goal setting process is to make your goals measurable. If your goal is to get more blog traffic, then I could visit your blog right now and you've already accomplished your goal. You need a number. How many hundreds, thousands, or millions of visitors do you want by the end of the year? How many extra visitors do you want this month? How much of an increase do you want for your blog's conversion rate? Most importantly, how will you make this happen?

Determining your "in-between zone" is a case by case basis. Some people have no problem with getting thousands of monthly visitors for their content. Other people are just starting out and dreaming of their first 100+ visitor months and eventually days.

A Growth Hack For Making Any Big, Measurable Goal Seem Possible

Want to get 100,000 monthly visitors? Who doesn't? Getting there is the hard part…if you think of it as going from 0 to 100,000. I recently learned that if you get 1,000 visitors every month, then you are just 8 doubles away from getting 100,000 monthly visitors. Here's the math:

Month #	Monthly Visitors
1	1,000
2	2,000
3	4,000
4	8,000
5	16,000
6	32,000
7	64,000
8	128,000

This is very important because you can use this approach for any measurable goal. Instead of going from 1,000 monthly visitors to 100,000 monthly visitors, all you need to do is go from 1,000 monthly visitors to 2,000 monthly visitors.

Making the jump each month will involve more work and possibly revenue on your part, but by viewing the steps on the staircase instead of a gigantic jump from the bottom of the staircase to the next floor, goals like these become more possible.

If you are just starting out, set the goal to double your blog traffic every month. If your goal is to go from 8,000 monthly visitors to 16,000 monthly visitors, don't view it as you needing an extra 8,000 monthly visitors. View it as doubling your total as "8,000 x 2" looks far less scary than "8,000 + 8,000."

The Preparation Stage

The doubling growth hack will work wonders by giving you a new perspective on what you need to do to accomplish your measurable goals.

However, this growth hack falls flat on its head if you don't have a plan to get there.

Will you double your blog traffic by writing more guest posts? How many more guest posts? Will you send more emails to your list? What about social media (don't worry. We'll discuss social media in greater detail in Part 3)? Do you plan on collaborating with your audience? What about repurposing your content?

These are just some of the tactics we've discussed. The challenge is determining which tactics you'll run with first, how to multiply their effects, and how to gradually add more tactics into the mix.

Before you map out your own journey, take a look at people who already accomplished your goal. If you want 100,000 downloads for your podcast episodes, read blog posts written by people who have achieved that goal. What did they do to get 100,000 downloads? What were some of their tactics and their overall strategies? Armed with this information, you can create a better map for yourself.

The Mapping Out Stage

With this quick preparation, you are now ready to map out your journey. During the Mapping Out Stage, I take out a piece of paper and write my current status on one end and my goal on the other. I then turn it into a timeline by dating the current status. Let's say a blogger got 8,000 visitors last month. That blogger would write down 8,000 visitors at the start of the 30 day timeline and 16,000 visitors at the end of the 30 day timeline.

Will you or I always double my blog traffic every month? No. However, even if a blogger goes from 1,000 monthly visitors to 1,500 monthly visitors, that same blogger is still on pace for 100,000 monthly visitors in 7 months assuming that blogger doubles the blog's traffic every month.

Within the rest of your timeline, identify all of the measurable tasks (i.e. "write 5 guest posts" instead of "write more guest posts") you'll need to accomplish to reach your goal. You're not identifying when you get them done, and order doesn't matter. As soon as you think of something, just write it on that sheet of paper. You can reorganize everything later on a different sheet of paper.

The mapping out stage identifies everything you believe will get you from where you are now to your desired goal. However, we still have to implement the plan to get the results.

The Implementation Stage

We do and don't do many things within our lives. A few principles drive us to take action, but desire and urgency will be your best friends in this stage. You must have a desire to perform the actions that you'll perform, and you must take advantage of urgency by creating daily, weekly, and monthly deadlines.

Let's say your goal for the month is to go from $2,500/mo to $5,000/mo. It's a big goal indeed, but if you believe in your ability to accomplish that goal and have a solid plan behind you, you can get it done.

If you determine that creating a training course will help you achieve that goal, you need to set various deadlines for that training course. With the monthly deadline in effect, you start by identifying the weekly deadlines:

Week 1: Create all training videos
Week 2: Edit and upload all training videos into the course

Week 3: Create the sales page

Week 4: Promote to your email list (on a specific date that you predetermine)

For the week that you're in, break it down even further into days. Here's an example of how you would break down Week 1.

Day 1: Outline the training course and determine how I'll record the videos

Day 2: Record videos for the first half of the training course

Day 3: Record videos for the second half of the training course

Day 4: Create supporting PDFs

Day 5: Upload all videos into Vimeo and have PDFs ready for upload into the course

Please note how I intentionally didn't mention Days 6 and 7. It's important to overestimate the amount of work you'll need to do. Different things may come up that require you to do certain things on Days 6 and 7. It may take you two days to complete the first half of the training course, but you aren't sweating it out because you gave yourself five days to accomplish a goal for the week.

Instead of spreading and cramming everything throughout the week, you have two free days that you can utilize if necessary. If you get everything done within the five day period, you can get a head start on Week 2.

Once you have this structure, all that's left to do is the actual work. I could easily turn this into a productivity book if I'm not careful, but I will say that waking up early and writing down what your day will look like on the night before (i.e. what are you doing tomorrow at 12 pm, and what about 5 pm? No guessing…just a firm answer that you stick to) will work wonders for your productivity.

The Delegation Stage

Just because a task is part of your Implementation Stage doesn't mean you have to do it. I take great joy in performing tasks such as creating training videos, writing content, and conducting podcast interviews. However, I don't do everything. I'm not editing my podcast episodes, uploading my videos to Vimeo, or editing my blog posts. I delegate those responsibilities to others.

There are plenty of places you can go to find quality help. My three favorite places to go for help are Fiverr, UpWork, and my own audience. I use Fiverr more as a one-off service where I get a book cover or training course logo. I use UpWork to find freelancers who can work with me more permanently. I don't always actively seek out people in my audience who can help (if you actively seek out people in your audience, that's not a bad thing at all), but when I interact with people in my audience, I sometimes think in the back of my mind, "This person would be perfect for that role."

Writing The Job Description

The job description you use will determine what kinds of applicants you'll get. Successful job descriptions are concise and clear as it's easier for applicants to read through your requirements and determine if your job is the right fit for them. It's important to help applicants figure this out early. A vague job description results in a stream of applicants, and you'll have to look through more applicants to find the one you want.

It's good to include bullet points in your job description and to utilize shorter paragraphs to make the description easier to read. In this case,

I didn't use bullet points but utilized small paragraphs and asked some important questions at the end.

> I am looking for someone who can edit videos to remove any mess ups and background noises (including clicks from my mouse). I will send you videos for my summit as I get them done. Upon hiring you, I'll send you some videos.

> You need to be fully available from May 20th to June 3rd. You won't be working countless hours during this two week period, but if I need you for something, I need you to be there within 6-12 hours during this timeframe. The only exception is if there's a timezone difference and you happen to be asleep when I'm sending you a message.

> I want someone who will do the videos quickly while maintaining quality so the work doesn't stockpile at the end. My summit takes place from June 7th to the 14th and I need the videos on Vimeo (you will have to upload them to my Vimeo account. Make sure the videos are PRIVATE).

> This project will end during the summit because at that time, the videos should all be in place. The earlier you get them done, the sooner I can get them on the site in preparation for June 7th to the 14th.

> If I like how you edit the videos for this summit, I will have you edit videos for future summits that I host (I'll host at least one more summit this year).

> When you edit videos, please write a list of edits you made within the video. I don't care how much or how little detail you go with

the list. Just make sure everything's on it so I know what you edited for a particular video.

In the job description, I make it clear when the videos need to be done by and to anticipate many incoming videos in the May 20th to June 3rd timeframe. Let your applicants know these types of dates upfront so they can plan out their calendars or not apply because your task won't work for them. It's better for the applicant to figure out this won't work and not apply than it is for you to figure out as you go deeper into the process.

I also required all applicants to answer four questions. I recommend having your applicants answer 3-5 questions because it's not too many, but that's enough questions to get a better idea of who is the right fit for the job.

1. What is your availability?—I want to make sure the May 20th to June 3rd timeframe works.

2. Do you have suggestions to make this project run successfully?—I want an applicant to get involved. The better the suggestions, the more likely I am to hire the applicant.

3. What questions do you have about the project?—I want to clear up any problems by inviting applicants to ask their questions. If it's a meaningful question, I know the applicant cares.

4. What past project or job have you had that is most like this one and why?—I want to see past experience that suggests the applicant is the right fit for the job.

I use UpWork to conduct most of my hires, and they have several good questions that you can choose from as well. I prefer to mix some of my questions with the questions that UpWork provides. Once you receive the applications, look through them and see who would be the best fit.

Create a list of 5-10 applicants who could fit the role and communicate with them even further. Get into a messaging conversation and then interview the top applicants. After the communication takes place, you can then make your hiring decision.

Upon that hiring decision, all you need to do now is train the employee through communication, videos, and/or documents on how they can best fulfill your job requirements. With your task now delegated, you'll have more time to expand in other areas of your content brand.

PART 3:

SOCIAL MEDIA MARKETING

You can't mention content marketing without mentioning social media marketing, and this form of marketing deserves its own chapter. Social media is the core platform brands use to increase their visibility and communicate with current customers. This tool can open the floodgates to traffic, opportunities, and sales.

However, just as it is possible to strike riches on social media, it's just as possible to constantly wander without achieving desirable results. Various social networks compete for your attention, and even when you hone in on a few, they are optimized to steal your minutes. The most successful social networks keep you on their sites for as long as possible. That's what they are supposed to do.

As you grow on social media, you must constantly break the temptation of continuously scrolling down, looking at trending topics, and getting absorbed in the unimportant things. Approach social media as a tool that you get on and leave as quickly as possible so you don't get distracted. While you're on social media, you need a game plan, and that game plan starts with an important decision.

Chapter 13:

CHOOSING YOUR SOCIAL NETWORK

The key to success on social media is to master a single social network, outsource most of the tasks for that social network, and then move onto the next social network. It's the simple concept of concentrating your time and effort towards one objective instead of spreading the same finite time and effort across 10 social networks.

Most people conduct their social media strategy like professional jugglers. They're juggling Twitter, Facebook, Instagram, YouTube, and six other social networks without any help. I know that if I tried juggling, I'd get overwhelmed and quickly watch all of the balls crash on the floor.

It's much easier to juggle a single ball than it is to juggle 10 of them. In fact, you wouldn't even call it juggling with one ball because it's an unfair advantage…an unfair advantage you need to utilize. I only started to master social media when I went on a social media hiatus. I chose to stick with Twitter, ignore the rest, and then I became successful on that platform.

Since the roads to success for each social network are very similar, my initial success on Twitter eventually rubbed off on the other social networks as I put in the time and effort. Over the upcoming pages, I'll share more information about each of the social networks. At the conclusion of this book, it's up to you to determine which social network you'll focus on. Forget about the rest until you master that one (I recommend committing 95% to 100% of your time on social media towards a single social network at this stage).

One Caveat

The social media world is constantly changing. It's a phrase that we hear so often because the truth behind that statement never changes. Some of my favorite social media and content marketing books failed to mention Facebook Live, an essential form of communication for anyone who's not afraid of the camera. Why? That's because Facebook Live wasn't a thing during the time those books were published.

A few years after this book's publication, new social networks will emerge and some social networks will die off. Remember Vine? As we move further away from Vine's death, more people who heard that word will think about plants than a social network that popularized short 6-second video loops.

By the time you read this book, a new social network may have established itself. Here's my advice for new social networks, regardless of the social network:

1. If you believe in that social network, aggressively pursue it on the exact day it becomes available. I did this with Periscope and got 2,000 followers on the first day. You get a big head start by aggressively pursuing a new social network early.
2. Integrate it into your other social networks so you drive traffic to your new content. This will give you an edge against other newcom-

ers who are trying to drive traffic to their content, or even worse, waiting for it to come.

3. Never depend on that social network. Use the new social network to attract people to your other social media accounts. Some Vine stars were just fine when the social network died because they had already used Vine to grow large followings on Twitter, Facebook, YouTube, and other social networks. Also, new social networks have a questionable shelf life in the beginning because even innovative ideas like Meerkat can get squashed by the big guys like Twitter's Periscope.

Now that I've addressed the caveat to dominating the social networks, it's time to take a deeper look at the top social networks.

Twitter—Many would start with Facebook when mentioning top social networks, but Twitter holds a special place for me. It's the social network that I first mastered, and looking back, Twitter is the easiest and least expensive social network to master.

Facebook—Let's face it. Facebook is the king of the social networks because it's a conglomerate of its own innovative ideas and innovative ideas from other social networks. As live videos gained prominence with the rise of Periscope, Facebook provided the Live Video functionality. As mentioned earlier, Vine died a while ago, but you may not remember that it was Instagram's 15 second loop videos (inspired by Vine) that did most of the killing. Those extra 9 seconds on an already popular social network ended Vine's reign. Facebook's done a ton of innovative things on their front such as offering Facebook Pages, Groups, and arguably the best advertising results on the planet. The biggest problem with Facebook is that more and more people see it as a pay to play social network where the content creator with the tight budget can't win.

Pinterest—You have to post a lot of pins on Pinterest to create highly engaging boards. However, if you don't want to create so many pins on Pinterest, there is a workaround. You can get contributors to post pins on your own boards. We'll cover this more in detail, but you basically get free posts from your community in a way that other social networks don't provide as of this publication.

YouTube—The best place to publish your videos. You can also publish videos on Vimeo, Facebook, and Twitter to give them an extra boost, but when people think about videos, they immediately think about YouTube.

Instagram—Facebook's partner in crime and social media killer. Instagram's 15 second loop videos arguably killed Vine, and Instagram Stories aim to turn SnapChat into a distant memory. Engagement is very strong on this platform in comparison to other platforms.

LinkedIn—It amazes me how little coverage this social network gets in the social media community. I still believe too many people view LinkedIn as the social network for finding a job. You're missing out on so much opportunity with that mindset. LinkedIn is a place where you can build meaningful relationships and publish (or republish) articles.

I'm not mentioning all of the social networks here. I predict SnapChat will either die or go through such rapid change that much of the content I write about SnapChat will get outdated or lose importance as the updates keep rolling in.

Chapter 14:

MASTERING TWITTER

Out of all of the social networks, Twitter is the easiest to master. Similarly to any social network, mastering Twitter will require a significant time commitment. That significant time commitment will only feel significant weeks, months, and years later because in a given day, mastering Twitter takes anywhere from 0-15 minutes per day (you get to 0 minutes per day as you delegate more Twitter related tasks).

The lifeline of your Twitter strategy is your ability to interact with your audience and provide them with the content they want. Determining what your audience wants isn't as hard as people make it out to be. You start with the assumption that your audience wants anything that you tweet. While this assumption is in play, only tweet content that matches up with your desired niche.

I love reading articles about running faster. However, I'm not sharing those on Twitter because my content brand resonates more with digital marketing and productivity. I'll share as many articles I can find or write about the top social networks, productivity hacks, and juicy content marketing tactics.

After tweeting under this assumption for a month, I look at my Twitter Analytics. These analytics give you access to a variety of statistics such as clicks per day, impressions per day, and daily growth. For this exercise, the section containing your most popular tweets matters more than any other section. When I first looked at my Twitter Analytics, I discovered that my Twitter related tweets get far more engagement than any other types of tweets. I took this knowledge and wrote more blog posts about Twitter. I then shared those blog posts more often than the non-Twitter related blog posts, and the result was more blog traffic.

However, just because something works now doesn't mean it will work forever. Eventually I saw an increase in engagement for my content marketing related blog posts. Twitter related blog posts still performed well, but not as well as their counterpart. Using this knowledge, I cut down on my Twitter related blog post production and doubled down on content marketing related blog posts. The result was more traffic.

You must continually anticipate what your audience wants, post as if they want everything that has your name on it, and then use Twitter Analytics to figure it out later. However, none of this matters if you have no followers or none of the right ones.

Growing A Targeted Audience

I got my first 100,000 Twitter followers before I graduated high school. No, I didn't buy a bunch of followers with my birthday money one year or become a Vine star. Rather, I followed a single tactic over and over again (following a single tactic or course of action is powerful because you can actually master it).

This one tactic is a modified version of the common advice "follow other people." A few words are missing from that phrase, and those words make the difference between dominating Twitter and just having a superficial number that serves no other purpose than a bragging point. Here's the modified phrase:

"Follow targeted people who are likely to follow you back."

I added seven words and replaced one…and now the tactic is completely different.

Gary Vaynerchuk doesn't try to convert people. He speaks to the people who have already been converted. I follow the same ideology. I'm not building an audience of random people and then persuading them to care about digital marketing. I build an audience of people who passionately care about digital marketing before they even know my name.

If you are reading this book, you are a part of my targeted audience. Chances are you heard about me before you bought the book, but if you didn't, then that's great too! I don't have to persuade you to accept content marketing or to fall in love with it. I can tell you want to dominate the content marketing landscape. You wouldn't be this far in the book if you weren't.

Now we need to address some critical questions…

#1: How do I find targeted people? Here's my follow-up question. Who or what content brand already has an audience filled with targeted people? Other digital marketing experts with a few hundred thousand extra followers than me already did the work and I follow their followers who are likely to follow back.

#2: How do I make sure they are likely to follow back? This is where various Twitter tools come in. Tools like StatusBrew, CrowdFire, Tweepi, and ManageFlitter make it easy for you to filter a user's followers by their follow ratio. In your search, you can filter for people who have a 100% follow ratio or something a little lower. That means you'll find a bunch of people interested in your niche who follow 500 people and are following 550 people. These people are far more likely to follow back than the people with 10,000 followers who only follow four people.

#3: What about the ratio? Growing your Twitter audience with this method almost guarantees your follower-to-following ratio will continuously go from looking mediocre to looking very good. On one day, you may have 5,000 followers and follow 5,200 people. As you continue to build your Twitter audience, you may have 5,500 followers and only follow 4,500 people. If you continuously unfollow the people who haven't unfollowed you within a week, you should be fine, but don't be afraid to temporarily sacrifice a good looking ratio for future gains later on.

Interacting With Your Audience

Most people use social media with a focus on the word media. You can tell people to read your blog posts and watch your latest videos, but if you don't interact with your audience, you miss out on a very important component of Twitter—and social media—success.

The easiest way to get a conversation rolling is to thank anyone who liked/retweeted one of your tweets or shared one of your pieces of content. To this day, I thank the people who share my content on Twitter and start a conversation. When I feel pressed for time, I'll like their tweets instead, but I want to show anyone who shares my content that I appreciate the act of them sharing my content.

It's an honor when anyone shares your content. The next time you share a social media post that you haven't pre-scheduled or made an evergreen post, ask yourself why you chose to share it. Ask yourself why you didn't just share something else instead. Asking yourself those two questions will give you a deeper appreciation for when someone decides to share your content in any form.

Turning Twitter Into An Opportunity Generating Machine

Thanking the people in your audience for sharing your content is a starting step to building quality conversations on Twitter. You can also use Twitter to connect with some of the top influencers in your niche. I can't count the number of podcast interviews and guest blogging opportunities that are *directly* related to Twitter let alone the indirect ones.

Sometimes people approached me. At other times, I approached them. In the beginning, you will need to do most of the approaching. As you continue to grow your Twitter audience and do great work, more people will approach you with those opportunities.

Since you'll start off by approaching people for these opportunities, our discussion will start in that area. The starting point is to get clear on which opportunities you want to pursue. Do you want guest blogging opportunities, podcast appearances, a little bit of both, or something entirely different? Then determine who can give you those opportunities… and who interacts with their followers.

Let's say you want to get on a podcast. More specifically due to my bias, you want to be a guest on my Breakthrough Success Podcast. It doesn't take much digging through my Twitter account to discover that I interact often with my followers. I also thank people for sharing my content as I mentioned earlier.

Want to get on my radar? Share my content and mention me @ MarcGuberti. If you build a strong enough relationship with me, do meaningful work, and ask me if you can get interviewed on my podcast, chances are I'll send you my calendar. I obviously can't guarantee this will work 100% of the time, but it works very often, and not just with me.

Interacting with people often puts you in their minds, and when they want to give someone an opportunity like a podcast appearance or guest blogging opportunity, you're one of the first people they'll think of. While you may not see much instant gratification from this form of interaction, it pays off greatly in the long-term.

Sometimes, however, you can get that instant gratification if you flip the conversation. Let's say you're the person with the opportunity and you're looking for people who would be a great fit. When I organized my Content Marketing Success Summit, I asked several people through Twitter if they would be interested in being speakers for the summit.

I knew some of these people for a long time. For others, that was the first they had heard of me. However, when people get an opportunity and have the time, they'll usually take it. I got enough speakers just from this one method that I used Twitter to land some speakers for my Productivity Virtual Summit and use it to this day to get guests for my Breakthrough Success Podcast.

To get opportunities from Twitter, or any other social network, you must be clear on which opportunities you want and have an idea of who can give them to you.

Evergreen Posting Cycle

On a typical day, I tweet over 100 times per day. It doesn't take me a single minute to write those tweets and schedule them out. That's because I have these tweets in an evergreen sequence that repeats over and over again. I can follow this approach because most of my blog's content is evergreen.

For instance, I checked my Twitter account while writing this part of the book (a big no-no, but I had to make an exception) and discovered my latest tweet was a blog post on getting more Instagram followers. That blog post will be relevant for a very long time if not forever. I also write blog posts that detail how people can become more productive and boost their confidence…two topics that will never go out of style.

I don't remember when I last scheduled that post. In fact, I almost never schedule posts anymore, and I don't even have a freelancer doing it for me anymore. I now use a social media tool called ViralTag to create evergreen posting cycles. I schedule all of the posts once, and instead of revisiting to rewrite and reschedule posts or upload a CSV file to HootSuite's bulk uploader, I no longer need to visit my ViralTag account. I only change things up when I write new content or want to drive more traffic to specific landing pages and types of content.

It's a set and forget system that handles the tweets for me so I can focus on other areas of my brand. I've entirely outsourced the growth of my Twitter audience as well, so all I manually do on that platform is interact with people. That's it.

Chapter 15:

MASTERING FACEBOOK

When you look at user base and revenue, Facebook is the leader of the pack. An unrivaled advertising system and the constant integration of innovations makes this social network one of the best ones available.

I say "one of the best" for a reason. Just because Facebook is the most popular social network doesn't mean it's the best one for you. This is similar to how I mastered Twitter first and how Vine stars emerged even when the former social network was still a few weeks old with only a few million users compared to other social networks with hundreds of millions of users at the time.

Facebook advertising is one of the most advanced forms of advertising on the planet, but also a challenging form of advertising to master. Due to the learning curve, I much prefer handing this responsibility to someone else and keeping a close look at my income.

If you decide to follow my route and have someone else do the Facebook ads for you, your two most important statistics are your costs per conversion and your earnings per conversion. If your average cost is $1 per conversion and your average earnings per conversion is $2 per conversion, then run that ad all day and night until those numbers change. Those ads literally pay for themselves.

Understandably, many people who take Facebook seriously also want to master Facebook ads. While the focus is placed on advertising, there are subtle ways to get your brand noticed on Facebook without paying a penny.

Facebook Live

Live videos are on fire right now. They allow content creators to shatter the 4th wall and interact with their audience in the moment as if you were having a casual conversation with one another. You can acknowledge your audience as your audience acknowledges you.

And Facebook rewards you mightily if you use their Live Video capability. The social network gives Live Videos a boost in the newsfeed over other types of posts. That means by doing a Live Video, you have a higher chance of getting seen by more people than if you just wrote a text post. Facebook grants this same power to videos published on Facebook even if they aren't live.

Facebook Groups

With Facebook ads stealing the show, there's an underrated but highly powerful feature in Facebook. It's an old feature that has been around for a while, but its power hasn't diminished. Rather, the importance of Facebook Groups has only grown due to Facebook's increasing shift towards a pay to play atmosphere.

Facebook Groups are the rebels in the pay to play atmosphere. You don't need any money to set up a group and get people in that group. Anytime something gets posted in the group, you get notified that a new post was posted in the group. That means even if people forget about your group for a while, a new post in the group shows up as a notification, and that lost member suddenly returns to the group.

Facebook Group Ideas

I first realized how powerful Facebook Groups were when I discovered that almost every $997+ training course seemed to offer a private Facebook Group as the bonus. If all of these training courses came with Facebook Groups, they had to be important. I then decided to create Facebook Groups for my own training courses and all other training courses after that.

You should create a Facebook Group for all of the people who buy a particular product. If you get people to buy a Fitness DVD, create a group so customers can talk about their stories and how much they exercised this week. People in the group who were slacking off will then get inspired and do one workout on the Fitness DVD every day.

Why does this matter? When you come out with Fitness DVD #2, you won't get sales from people who bought Fitness DVD #1 but never took action. You need these people to take action so they are more likely to buy your future products.

The first time I seriously used Facebook Groups for my brand was when I hosted the first Content Marketing Success Summit. I created two groups for the summit. The first group was for all summit attendees and the second group was for all of my partners.

Both of those groups were important because they allowed me to communicate with my audience on one of the most popular social network on the planet. To grasp the power of this communication, remember that Facebook will notify you in the Notifications Tab when something gets posted in the group.

When new sessions came out for the Content Marketing Success Summit, I posted a schedule in the Facebook Group and some of my thoughts. This strategy created more excitement around the summit and helped seal more All-Access Pass sales. On the partners side, I posted all of the swipe copy in the Partners Group Page and got everyone excited with a leaderboard based on who brought in the most All-Access Pass sales. The top two winners got an Echo Dot, and the sense of competition plus the constant reminder of the leaderboard brought in more sales.

I emailed all of this information to my attendees and partners respectively, but having the Facebook Groups in place gave me another medium of communication and a place where members could interact with one another.

Another idea I've seen is a public Facebook Group which consists of a community of people interested in your niche. As the group's founder, you appear as an instant leader and authority, and you can generate a lot of traffic and engagement from this type of group.

I am part of a podcasting community group where podcasters frequently ask and answer questions that get posted in the group. Several relationships get formed within this group. If you create one of these groups, you have the option to pin a post to the top of the feed that appears at the top of the group's feed.

You can use this pinned post to promote a blog post, landing page, or something you've been working on. Changing this pinned post up every once in a while and getting thousands of members into your group will result in a consistent stream of traffic to the content you pinned to the top of the group.

Chapter 16:

MASTERING PINTEREST

Pinterest is one of the dark horses of the social media landscape. Pinterest's categorized eye candy layout keeps users on the site for several hours. While Pinterest was once primarily viewed as a lady's social network (at one point, 80% of Pinterest users were women), an influx of men have joined the social network. In some primetime regions, the split is close to 50-50.

Pinterest is an amazing traffic source if utilized properly. Kristin Larsen of the Believe In A Budget Blog saw her traffic go from 5,000 page views to over 40,000 page views in a single month after incorporating Pinterest into her promotional strategy. Four months later, her blog was hovering towards 200,000 monthly page views. She provides more details in her blog post "Pinterest Case Study: Why You Don't Need Pinterest Followers," and note that she achieved all of those results with just 2,700 Pinterest followers.

You don't need a ton of followers on Pinterest to make a big splash. At a time when I had 500 followers, one of my pins got repinned over 1,000 times. That's the viral potential of Pinterest, and this growth can happen to anyone at anytime, regardless of how many followers you have on Pinterest.

How To Schedule Your Pins In Advance

When Pinterest was new, there were a plethora of Twitter tools but no comparable tools for Pinterest. Scheduling pins was a difficult luxury to come across, and many services charged a premium to get the privilege to schedule pins.

ViralWoot changed that when they introduced scheduling pins. It was basic at the time, but it worked and allowed people to schedule their own pins. ViralWoot still allows you to schedule a limited number of pins for free before asking you to pay a premium. ViralWoot is great for getting your feet in the water. ViralTag, the tool I also use for Twitter, allows you to truly embrace Pinterest's power.

ViralTag allows you to schedule pins and set up an evergreen posting cycle which is very useful. You won't have to worry about pins getting scheduled because you can place your scheduled evergreen pins into the evergreen posting cycle. You can target individual boards with this approach or pin the same pin onto multiple boards in a continuous cycle.

If you don't like the idea of scheduling many pins in advance, you can hire someone else to perform that role. My recommendation is to schedule some pins on your own before hiring someone so you know how to craft better instructions, but once you know how to schedule pins, feel free to have someone else do it.

Hiring someone to handle the evergreen posting cycles is more useful for Pinterest than for Twitter because you can have multiple evergreen posting cycles for Pinterest. On Pinterest, you have multiple boards to manage while you only need to manage one evergreen posting cycle for

Twitter since you can't categorize content on Twitter like you can with Pinterest.

Group Boards Present The Ultimate Advantage

If you pin the same pin over and over again on the same board, will your followers get annoyed by repetition? If you have contributors on your board, then that's not a problem. Your contributors will fill your group board with unique pins, and you can post the same few pins every day. I do recommend setting up a few different pins instead of a single pin in your evergreen cycle, but getting contributors to arm your boards up with valuable pins will make the pin creation process much smoother for you.

And did I mention your audience will skyrocket?

As contributors continue to post pins to your group board, your boards will rank higher and attract more attention from Pinterest's search engines. In addition, Pinterest's following mechanism works differently from all social networks. When someone follows you, they click "Follow All" which means that user follows all boards on that person's profile. That also includes group boards that the person is a part of (for instance, your group board). This allows your individual group boards to reap more followers and provide you with a platform where you can share your content to an even larger audience.

However, why just stop at creating group boards? Many group boards with 10,000+ followers need your pins if you specialize in the right niche. Even if you have zero followers, you can get your pins on these group boards and get your pin in front of 10,000 people. Talk about an overnight growth hack!

The challenge with that tactic is finding the group boards and becoming a contributor. Finding group boards is surprisingly easy. Here are the steps you need to take:

#1: Search "[Your niche] group board" on Pinterest. For instance, I would search something like "Social Media Group Board."

#2: Make sure you click "Boards" as Pinterest has the "All Pins" option selected by default. Once you click "Boards," you will then see a bunch of boards that accept contributors.

Once you find the list of group boards, you can proceed by commenting on a pin from the group board's owner (when you see the pictures of contributors, look for the first picture to the left. That's the group board's owner) or finding that owner's website and leaving a message in the contact form. Some of these contact forms also provide an email address, and it's ideal to use the email address for two reasons:

#1: The inbox is a better communication method than Pinterest.

#2: You don't know if the contact form is broken (some appear fine but are really broken), but the email address is a surefire guarantee.

Some will say yes while others will say no, but the only way you get people to say yes is by contacting many people and accepting rejection as part of the process towards the ultimate goal. Then you'll have the ability to communicate with thousands of additional followers overnight. You won't see those thousands of extra followers populating your profile, but you can share your content with that audience.

What Kinds Of Pictures Win

On the Pinterest landscape, millions of newly published pins compete for attention. The picture you use plays a big role in how much engagement your pin generates. Pinterest's design will shrink wide pictures and make them less appealing.

However, Pinterest doesn't have a cap for how long a picture can be. This concept explains why infographics dominate most people's Pinterest feeds. Infographics are the lengthy pictures that contain information that looks like an advanced outline for a blog post. The combination of pictures and informative text makes infographics appealing to the eye and, as a result, grabs our attention. Canva is a popular tool for creating infographics, but you can also create a lengthy infographic with PowerPoint and KeyNote. You can export any slide as an image and then upload that image to Pinterest.

Regardless of which tool you use to create your infographics, success comes with infographics that work. Instead of guessing what type of infographic would win, browse through Pinterest and see which types of infographics win. Is the infographic filled with words or just a few quick tips. Are there plenty of pictures within the infographic or just 2-3? The traits of success infographics have slight variations within different niches, but many of them combine text with plenty of pictures that highlight concepts or tell a story.

Some pinners will leverage infographics with the addition of themed pictures. Themed pictures all have the same background scheme and text. Anytime you share one of your blog posts, podcast episodes, or videos, utilize a themed picture. To take this a step further, have the theme match with your content. If your blog has a blue background, make sure your picture has a blue background. Use the same font for each picture you use to promote any of your blog posts. If you insert a picture within the image, insert that picture at the same location for each of these pins.

Themed pins will help your followers more easily recognize your content. If those same people associate your content with value, you can rest assured that theming your pins will result in more engagement and traffic back to your content.

Chapter 17:

MASTERING YOUTUBE

YouTube is the 800 pound gorilla in the room. People either focus on it or don't spend any time growing their channel. When most people talk about SEO, Google gets the spotlight. However, YouTube is also one of the top websites in existence, and since it's owned by Google, the social network built on videos receives a ton of love from Google. In addition to this support, YouTube also stands strong as its own search engine which helps over a billion monthly visitors find the videos they want to watch.

Not only are these visitors coming back to YouTube often, but these are engaged visitors who stay on YouTube for a long period of time. YouTube users stay on the site for over 10 minutes at a time. If some of these visitors enjoy watching your YouTube videos, then they will certainly come back for more. To explore YouTube further, we'll cover the three areas that matter the most for your success on YouTube.

#1: Subscribers

A large quantity of quality subscribers is the best type of audience to have on YouTube. Quality subscribers are people who are pre-determined to be interested in your niche. These people are subscribed to YouTube channels related to your niche and want to watch numerous videos about your area of expertise.

Getting more subscribers comes down to crafting an appealing channel combined with the right marketing. Having an audience outside of YouTube helps, but it isn't required. You can leverage other people's audiences via interviewing your niche's experts, commenting on other people's videos, and other means. But when you decide to leverage other people's audiences, the only way you will become successful with this method is to take a win-win approach.

Commenting gives you more exposure. Your comments will also give the videos more exposure and social proof. It's a win-win. Interviewing other experts within your niche gives you more credibility and exposure (if the expert promotes the interview) and the expert gets more exposure as well. That's a win-win too. There are many ways to get more subscribers. The key thing is to find a few methods that work very well for you and then capitalize on them.

Here's a list of 20 methods you can utilize to grow your channel's subscriber base:

1. **Upload more videos**. People will need to watch multiple videos on your channel before they decide to subscribe to your channel.
2. **Include a channel trailer**. In 1-2 minutes, tell people what kind of videos you upload on YouTube, and share your credibility.
3. **Tweet your videos**. By tweeting your videos and getting some of your followers to view your videos, you will get more subscribers.
4. **Pin your videos and scatter those pins across different boards**. You can watch a YouTube video on Pinterest without leaving the social network. However, you want people to leave Pinterest so

they can subscribe to your channel. In the description, mention that there are more videos on your channel which you can get to by clicking on a link in the description so they can subscribe to your channel.

5. **Have a YouTube subscribe button on your blog**. By having a YouTube subscribe button on your blog, you can get a new subscriber without forcing someone to leave your blog. That way, you get a new subscriber and that individual stays on your blog a little longer.

6. **Have a "click here to subscribe" annotation on the corner of all of your videos**. Have the annotation link to a subscription confirmation for your channel. All you need to do is paste the link in the box and from the drop down options, choose "subscribe." By doing this, anyone who clicks on the annotation automatically gets subscribed to your channel.

7. **Urge people to subscribe to your channel, but don't beg**. Urging people in the proper way can be done by saying, "If you enjoyed this video, then please subscribe to my channel which I update every week about social media, business, and blogging." Begging is just saying, "Please, please, pretty please subscribe to my YouTube channel."

8. **Post your videos on Facebook**. Some of your friends will end up subscribing to your YouTube channel. It is important to interact with the fan base that you have already built in order to get more subscribers for your channel.

9. **Consistently publish videos**. If you post videos on a consistent basis, people will notice and subscribe to your channel.

10. **Let people know when you publish your videos**. I let everyone know that I publish my videos every Saturday at 9 am Eastern. That

means all of my subscribers (maybe not all of them) are constantly refreshing my channel every Saturday at 8:59 am Eastern.

11. **Post videos on a frequent basis**. Posting consistently isn't enough. When I decided to publish 1 YouTube video every week, I saw a dramatic increase in the number of subscribers I got for my channel. If you are publishing 1 YouTube video every week, you will give your subscribers more to watch, and they will be back for more. Publishing 1 YouTube video every year is still being consistent, but you need to combine consistency with frequency.

12. **Properly tag your videos**. Use phrases that you would want people to search for in order to find your videos. If your video is about getting more retweets, use tags like "how to get more retweets on Twitter."

13. **Write good titles for your videos**. In your title, you need to tell people what your video is about. The longer the title, the better. However, make sure your title is under 110 characters so people can still tweet your video using a link shortener.

14. **Write optimized descriptions**. The ideal description is one that has 2-3 paragraphs and has a link at the bottom to subscribe to your channel. Instead of simply sending people to your channel with this link, you can send them to a link that automatically subscribes the person who clicks on the link.

15. **Create quality videos**. Creating a script or outline, having the right lighting, and no unexpected sounds in the background all help, but nothing beats practice.

16. **Interact with the subscribers that you already have**. The subscribers that you already have can tell their friends about you. By inter-

acting with your subscribers, you will be getting more subscribers via word of mouth.

17. **Have a strategic channel background**. The channel background should be a picture of you at your profession or something that relates to your niche.

18. **Subscribe to other people's YouTube channels**. Some of these people will subscribe back to your channel while others will interact with you.

19. **Comment on other people's videos**. This will give you backlinks on YouTube which allows you to rank higher on YouTube's search results.

20. **Fill in the blank**. That's not a typo. As the years go by, more tactics will become available. Choose a tactic that works for you. You might decide to utilize Facebook ads or to attend offline events to grow your YouTube channel. Any book is meant to expand your horizon, and I encourage you to expand your horizons as you implement the insights in this book.

#2: Minutes Watched

YouTube has made it a point to emphasize that they consider minutes watched before they consider the number of views your video gets. Part of this is to combat spam. Anyone can buy 100,000 views, and even if these people only stayed on the video for 10 seconds or less, they get counted as viewers. These bogus views make a video look better to a potential viewer. However, these same videos are not likely to show up high in YouTube's search results.

If you want to rank high, then you need to get people to watch as many minutes of your videos as possible. There are two main ways to achieve this objective.

The first method is to create compelling videos that make someone naturally interested in watching your entire video. But what makes a compelling video? The playing field is slightly different for each person. See what your competitors are uploading to YouTube and analyze what works. Then, as you create your own videos, take a look at your videos' retention rates so you get an idea of which videos are getting the most attention. You don't want to look at a video's audience retention rate until it has surpassed 100 views. If you base your retention rate on eight views, then you don't have enough data to make a firm conclusion.

The second method still requires you to create a compelling video, but the length of your video is also a factor. Retention rate plays a role in how much of the video someone actually watches, but the number of minutes watched is more important.

Sometimes, if I want one of my particular videos to do very well, I'll make it longer. I will come up with more case studies and key points to discuss. I extensively plan out the video while most of my other videos just take five minutes of planning.

My longest video as of writing is a little over 43 minutes long. With the help of advertising, people watched that video for over 378,000 minutes. As of my finding that statistic, the video had a total of 31,838 views. The average person viewed the video for 11 minutes and 53 seconds.

Another video I published, The 4 Core Beliefs Of All Highly Productive People, will rarely have a viewer who watches the video for 11 minutes and 53 seconds. That video is only 8 minutes and 50 seconds long, so one viewer would have to watch the same video twice (or stop halfway during the second view) for that view to exceed 11 minutes and 53 seconds.

The average view duration for this particular video is 3 minutes and 22 seconds. For the sake of math, let's say my longer video averages 12 minutes per viewer and my productivity video averages 4 minutes per viewer. If 1,000 people view each video for the average amount of time, here are the numbers:

> Longer video: 12,000 minutes watched
> Productivity video: 4,000 minutes watched

It doesn't matter if they both had the same number of views. What matters is that people spend more time watching one video than the other. Even if the Productivity video had a 100% retention rate, the longer video still performs better in minutes watched. Make compelling videos, but also see how you can make them longer to get more minutes watched.

5 Ways To Increase Minutes Watched

Getting people to spend more time watching your videos is important for your channel's success. With that in mind, here is a list of ways you can increase the amount of time people stay engaged with your videos.

1. **Get more people to subscribe to your channel**. According to the YouTube Creator Academy, subscribers watch your videos longer than anyone else.

2. **Have a professional introduction**. Your introduction is the deciding point of your YouTube videos. The more professional your

introduction is, the more people will enjoy your video. Professional introductions intro you and your video's topic in 10-15 seconds.

3. **Have an incredible channel trailer**. When people visit your channel for the first time, they need an enticing reason to watch your videos. An incredible channel trailer that sums up you and your channel will result in more subscribers and minutes watched.

4. **Mix short and long videos**. Would you rather watch a 1 hour video or a 1 minute video? The shorter your videos are, the more likely people will be to watch to the end. However, some people will watch the hour long video to the end, so it's best to utilize both approaches to increase your channel's overall minutes watched.

5. **Show people that you are popular**. Most people still believe viewership has a big impact on how YouTube ranks videos. In addition, most people think that popularity is measured by the number of views a YouTube video has. If your YouTube videos have thousands of views, people will watch those videos from start to finish just because thousands of other people have watched those videos as well. With that said, buying views is a bad practice that will hurt your ranking on YouTube, so you need to earn every view you get.

#3: Consistency Of Video Uploads

The more consistent you are with your video uploads, the more likely you are to get noticed by your subscribers. The thing about uploading and publishing videos is that some of your subscribers have opted to get notified via email. Every time you publish a new video, an email blast gets sent to a large group of your subscribers.

Subscribers will remember who you are if you consistently upload YouTube videos. If you upload a YouTube video every week at the same time, then your subscribers will remember you.

Some of these subscribers will constantly check your channel to see what you came out with next. Subscribers like that will engage with your video and watch it. Those actions will cause your video to surge in YouTube's rankings and get more search engine traffic as well. Your subscribers are the people who get the ball rolling. But in order for them to get the ball rolling, they must remember you, and you must upload videos consistently.

10 Tactics To Come Up With More YouTube Video Ideas

The key to combining consistency and frequency is to have enough video ideas and then taking action on those ideas. Taking action requires that you remove as many possible hazards to entry as possible. For instance, if it takes you an hour to set up your studio to record a single video, you'll have a lot of resistance preventing you from starting the video. If it just takes you 1-2 minutes to setup for a video, you'll have less resistance and therefore create more videos.

Your video setup won't matter if you don't have the ideas in place. To combat that issue, you can utilize these 10 tactics to come up with more YouTube video ideas.

1. **Look at your blog posts**. If you write one blog post every day and publish one YouTube video every week, you will have seven times as many blog posts as you have YouTube videos. That means you already have the ideas in front of you. Just take one of your blog posts and turn it into a YouTube video!

2. **Look at other people's blog posts**. See how you can combine your knowledge with someone else's blog posts to create an original You-Tube video. Reading other people's blog posts will also expand on your knowledge.

3. **Talk about a problem in your niche**. People want to know the common pitfalls in your niche so they know to avoid them. In addition to talking about the problems in your niche, be sure to provide the solutions for each of those problems.

4. **Talk about success stories**. Chances are there is someone inspirational in your niche who has gone through a lot in order to become successful. You can create a success story for that individual and show others that they can be successful too.

5. **Talk about your own experiences**. You may have a success story of your own or just want to talk about what happened to you yesterday. Regardless of what you talk about, you need to connect it back to your niche.

6. **Look at other people's YouTube videos**. Looking at other people's YouTube videos will allow you to identify what kinds of videos people in your niche are uploading and which ones are the most popular uploads. This can help you identify which videos you need to publish on YouTube.

7. **Look at your past YouTube videos**. Maybe you shared a tip in one of your YouTube videos that you want to expand on. It's also possible that you liked the message in one of your first videos but don't like the way it came out (it takes a while to get experience). You can create a Part 2 or a better version of an older video.

8. **Any new updates relating to your niche**. People who want to learn more about your niche do their best to stay up to date. When

something big happens in your niche, you can come out with a new YouTube video explaining what just happened.

9. **Tips about anything related to your niche.** Many viewers are looking for good nuggets of information. Providing tips about anything related to your niche gets the job done.

10. **Core values.** Whether these are the core values to living a happier life or getting more Twitter followers, talking about them and including "Core Values" in your video's title will attract attention (i.e. 5 Core Values All Productivity Experts Share).

7 YouTube Mistakes To Avoid So You Can Smoothly Sail The Horizon

The impact a successful YouTube channel has on a brand can no longer be questioned. The social media behemoth attracts over 1 billion unique visitors to its platform every month, and some YouTubers now generate full-time incomes because of this traffic. With success stories of certain channels bringing in six figure incomes, more people have looked at YouTube as a way to market their brands. However, as more people use YouTube from a business standpoint, more methods get mixed up and misconceptions lead to mistakes. These are seven mistakes that you must avoid so you continue to grow on YouTube.

#1: Not Uploading Enough Videos

Uploading YouTube videos at a consistent rate allows your channel to remain active and give your subscribers a good experience. The moment you stop uploading YouTube videos at a consistent rate, you will lose some of your subscribers, and your account's growth will halt. In order to avoid the stagnation of your account's growth, you must upload numerous videos at a consistent rate. The amount of videos you should upload depends on your channel and style. With that said, every YouTuber should upload and publish one video every week. Some people may feel capable of uploading and publishing two YouTube videos every week. The more YouTube videos you upload to your channel, the more choices you give your subscribers and potential subscribers. While you give your audience more options, you must ensure value in all of your videos. If the people in your audience do not appreciate the options you made available for them, then they will look for someone else. On YouTube, it is easy for someone to find videos just like yours. That is why your first impression in terms of value is so important for doing well on YouTube.

#2: Exclusively Uploading Short Videos

For some people, uploading short YouTube videos is their style. However, the longer videos tend to perform better on YouTube's search engine. Longer videos tend to outperform shorter videos because YouTube uses minutes watched as an essential metric to rank its videos. It is better from a SEO standpoint when a visitor watches 10 minutes of a one hour video than it is when someone watches a three minute video from start to finish. Retention rate matters too, but the minutes watched metric is more significant for YouTube SEO.

#3: Bad Audio

The audio of your videos has an impact on how people perceive your channel and brand. If you have bad audio in your videos, people will find it difficult to listen to your videos even if you offer great advice or good humor. The way your videos sound is just as important as the value you provide within those videos. If you don't have any microphone, then your audio is decent at best. I use the Yeti Microphone for my videos, and many of the highly successful YouTubers use the microphone for their YouTube videos and training courses.

#4: Not Asking For Subscribers Or Comments

At the end of every YouTube video, don't be afraid to ask your audience to subscribe and comment. The best way to get something is to ask for it, but you don't want to beg either. There is a difference between saying "Please subscribe" and "Please, please, please subscribe." I have an annotation that shows up during all of my videos enticing people to subscribe, and at the end of my videos, I encourage interaction and subscriptions. I want to make sure the people who appreciated my video the first time can easily get notified about my other videos and have a conversation with me.

#5: Branching Out Too Far On One Channel

As you get more experience with uploading and publishing videos, it will become tempting to branch out and create a broad channel. Creating a broad channel is one of the worst mistakes to make on YouTube. When you make a broad channel, your channel's identity becomes hazy, and that will result in fewer subscribers. Let's say you upload some videos about sports, some videos about fashion, and some videos about gadgets. It would be difficult to gain an audience with that channel because viewers won't know what niche your channel fits into. Instead of creating one broad channel, create a series of specific channels with one clear niche.

By creating channels with clear niches, it will be easier for you to build a strong following on YouTube.

#6: Not Breaking Your Channel Into Categories

As you upload more videos, you will get into specific areas within your niche. Getting into specific areas within your niche will fulfill specific needs and desires that your viewers have. However, your viewers won't want to scroll through all of your videos to find specific topics. You can make it easier for your viewers to find what they want by breaking your channel into categories.

I have a digital marketing channel, but since there are various components that go towards successful digital marketing, I create different categories based on the videos I have done. I have a social media category and a blogging category because I know that some of my subscribers care more about my social media advice and other subscribers care more about my blogging advice. Breaking my channel into categories makes it easier for both of those subscribers to find what they are looking for in a time effective manner.

#7: Not Sharing Your YouTube Videos On Your Other Social Networks

Just because you put a video on YouTube does not guarantee it will get thousands of views let alone a few million. In order to get more views from YouTube's search engine, you must generate some of the buzz on your own. When I upload a new YouTube video, I always tweet and promote that video on my other social networks. I even promote some of those videos to my email list. Share your YouTube videos with the audience you have already built so more people see the video. That way, the initial momentum from your audience will allow your video to expand. That expansion will help you grow your audience.

YouTube is still a leading social network, and optimizing it for your brand's growth will put you in contact with a new audience. You can use the audience you already built to jumpstart your YouTube channel's growth. By avoiding these common mistakes, YouTube growth will be smooth sailing, and the results will be more impactful for your business.

Chapter 18:

MASTERING INSTAGRAM

How hot is Instagram for businesses? The social network boasts over 300 million daily active users, and the average Instagram posts greatly exceed the engagement of the average post on other social networks. Brands are scrambling to master Instagram as quickly as possible. They want large, targeted, and active audiences who will fall in love with their pictures and products.

But how can we master Facebook's partner in crime? How do we build audiences of people who engage with our pictures and go to our content off Instagram? That's what we will explore in this chapter.

7 Ways To Get Targeted Instagram Followers

The rules for Instagram are similar to the rules for any other social network. By noticing the subtle differences, you can take your Instagram growth from good to great. These tactics will lead you to victory.

#1: Follow The Right People

You could technically follow many Follow4Follow accounts to increase your following. However, those followers are more interested in adding you to their own list of follows than your content.

You don't want an audience of real, yet non-targeted and non-interested followers. Rather, you should be looking to build an audience of targeted individuals who have a strong interest in your brand. Here's how you find those people:

- Find a person in your niche with a big audience.
- Go to that person's most recent post.
- Follow the people who liked that photo.
- Repeat the process with more influencers' accounts.

While Instagram requires a few additional steps compared to the Twitter approach, you'll be following people who are:

- Interested in your niche.
- Active.
- Engaging with content related to your niche.

Making a careful selection of who to follow will help you build a relevant audience that engages with your content. Try to be sure that the people you follow will be likely to follow you back.

Not only is it possible to find targeted and engaged users who are likely to follow you back, it's also easy.

#2: Like The Right Pictures

Google the phrase "how to get more Instagram followers" and you'll come across the tip I previously mentioned: follow users who like content related to your niche. More people are clicking on particular images to see who has liked them, then following those users.

This is a method people use to gain like-minded followers. Not only can you follow people who liked the image, but you can also do the liking.

By liking hundreds of pictures related to your niche, you will put you in front of thousands of potential targeted followers.

Like photos posted by influencers in real time. The sooner you like the picture, the more exposure you'll get. If you know an influencer posts pictures at a certain time each day, log into Instagram at that time so you can be one of the first people to like the post.

#3: Post Consistently

Engaging with other people's pictures and following their active users will put your account in front of more people. But unless your account makes an impression on visitors, you won't get many followers.

Posting consistently makes your account more impressive. Consistent posting makes it clear to potential followers that you are an active user. Until recently, there was no free way to schedule your Instagram posts. Now you can get the job done with HootSuite, but keep in mind that you must be logged in to the Instagram app in order to post it. HootSuite doesn't actually schedule the Instagram post. Rather, it notifies you to post to Instagram according to your schedule. So if you schedule a post for 6 pm, but don't log into Instagram for the entire day, your picture won't get posted.

Posting consistently on Instagram requires a bit more work, but it is also more rewarding. Far more people engage with Instagram posts than with Twitter and Facebook posts. I have two predictions: the first is that the scheduling problem won't last very long. My second prediction is that Instagram will keep growing, and you'll want to post consistently now and let other people complain about the technological restraints.

#4: Optimize Your Bio

Let people know what you do professionally, and who you are personally. List some of your personal interests and professional accomplishments. People who have never heard of you before should immediately get a sense of who you are just by reading your bio.

And no bio is complete without a link to your blog or website. This link will help you increase your traffic from Instagram, and that traffic can equate to subscribers and sales. So should you link to your post or landing page?

If you post your blog post pictures on Instagram and want people to read your content, simply include "Read this post by clicking the link in my bio" at the end of the post description.

If you prefer to include your blog's link within your Instagram post descriptions, link to your landing page in the bio. Social media is a means to an end.

Successful Instagram users aren't getting more followers just for the sake of having a pretty number and bragging rights. The purpose of Instagram varies for each person. Some people view Instagram as a way of building an audience and getting more blog traffic, while others want to funnel as much of their Instagram traffic to their landing pages as possible.

If you are using Instagram to grow your email list, then why link to your blog? Link to one of your landing pages to expedite your main objective. Of course, if you view Instagram only as a means to an end and don't bother interacting with your audience, your Instagram experience won't be a smooth one. No matter which social network you use, interaction is a must.

#5: Include Hashtags

Use Hashtags to get your content found on Instagram. They're the SEO for Instagram. Choose the right hashtags and your pictures will get in front of all of the people searching for that hashtag.

I like to use at least three hashtags in a given Instagram post. Before I choose hashtags, I'll put the hashtag into Instagram's search engine to see how they rank. When choosing my Instagram hashtags, I'll mix in the most popular hashtags with hashtags that aren't as popular. Often less popular hashtags still get a lot of visibility. Getting a lot of engagement for those hashtags boosts social proof and helps out with the more popular hashtags.

#6: Comment On Other People's Pictures

Here's a fun activity. Find a successful Instagram picture related to your niche. Then see how many people liked the picture and how many people commented. I decided to do this with one of my pictures:

> 41 likes
>
> 2 comments

Foundr Magazine is crushing it on Instagram. I decided to look at the stats of one of their Zig Ziglar pictures:

> 5,021 likes
>
> 34 comments

Why does this fun and insightful game help you obtain more Instagram followers? Instagram pictures don't get nearly as many comments as likes, which makes the comments section an easier place to stand out.

Post a meaningful comment, and you'll get more followers from that person's audience.

When I got these stats, Foundr Magazine had over 800,000 Instagram followers. One of their case study posts at the time only had five comments. If you find an opportunity like this and write Comment #6, you are automatically exposed to thousands of people. You won't get in front of Foundr Magazine's entire audience (or another successful brand's audience depending on where you write your comment), but a few thousand people seeing your comment isn't so bad.

#7: Post Awesome Pictures

Not all pictures are created equal. In the end, there are only three types of pictures that I post on my Instagram account.

The first type is something personal. I like it when people can connect with me on a more personal level. I've had numerous conversations with my audience about running, dogs, and the Red Sox. I love those types of conversations. Not only does my audience get to know me better, but I get to know them better, too.

The second type of picture is a motivational quote. I like to inspire my audience so much that, to shift gears a little bit, I created an inspirational quotes board on Pinterest that currently has over 4,000 pins. I am that serious about inspiring others (to be fair, I've got almost 600 contributors helping me with that board).

The third type of picture I post is a picture of one of my blog posts in order to drive more traffic to my blog. Make sure you use a similar theme for each of your blog post related pictures so your followers recognize your blog post pictures from other pictures that will show up in their feeds.

Understand what types of pictures you want to craft and make them epic. For personal pictures, I like candid shots take in the moment. I hire a freelancer for blog pictures and motivational quotes because I prefer to do other things than create and choose those pictures.

5 Ways To Get More Blog Traffic From Instagram

Ever get random blog traffic? It's a mixed feeling of excitement and the question, "What can I do to get more traffic from that source?" One day, I was surprised by Instagram traffic to my blog.

I followed targeted people on Instagram to grow my account. One day, I noticed that Instagram brought 10 people over to my blog that same day. Ten visitors a day adds up to 3,650 new visitors each year. I wasn't doing cartwheels over an additional 10 daily visitors, but neither did I discount the potential for Instagram to increase my blog traffic.

In fact, I did those cartwheels precisely because those visitors came from Instagram. At the time, my last Instagram post was two months old, and the one prior to that was almost a year old. I attracted 10 people to my blog with (at the time) an inactive Instagram account. I knew that if it was an active account with a more targeted audience, the results would be much better. Today my blog is consistently getting more traffic from Instagram, and that traffic is growing. Here are five tips you can utilize to grow your blog with Instagram.

#1: Link To Your Blog In Your Bio

This is how I got my initial 10 visitors. I followed people, they followed me back, and some of those people decided to check out my blog. I was also experimenting with a second method for growing a targeted and active audience (but more on that in a second).

Linking to your blog in your bio is perhaps the easiest way to increase traffic. It takes a few seconds and requires little to no effort. All you do is edit your bio and add a link to your blog. It's that easy!

#2: Grow A Targeted And Active Audience

There are many ways to grow an audience on Instagram. Many sites out there offer a myriad of ways to grow your Instagram fans. Some suggest buying followers, but that is a big no-no.

I am more interested in methods that will actually result in an audience of people who are interested in my pictures and ready to engage with my posts. And you should be too.

Build a targeted and active audience by hanging out where the targeted and active people hang out. How? First, find an influencer in your niche with a big audience. Next, visit the influencer's account and look at his or her latest post and who has engaged with, or liked it. Finally, follow all of those people.

It's that easy. People liked the picture because they were interested in that topic (your niche). These people are likely active and engaged on the platform, so this simple follow strategy will help you build your own audience.

#3: Post Pictures Of Your Latest Blog Post

The day I received 10 visitors from Instagram to my blog I did not include an image from my latest blog post. But if I had, I would have easily doubled my visitors. Posting pictures of your latest blog posts on Instagram is a creative way to use the platform to increase your blog traffic.

#4: Post Pictures Made To Spread

If I share a motivational quote on Instagram, it doesn't usually result in a direct increase in my blog traffic. If anything, I'll receive an indirect increase in traffic because some curious people will click on my blog link.

These types of posts are designed more for spreading power than traffic power. The stronger your image's spreading power, the more people that image reaches. Motivational quotes happen to perform very well on virtually every social network. These pictures normally get a lot of engagement and attract followers.

This means my blog post images are seen by a larger audience. Motivational quote pictures motivate others and increase my following, which brings more attention to the blog post images that drive my traffic.

#5: Spend Extra Time Making The Pictures Look Nice

Each picture you put on your Instagram profile needs at least 10 minutes of care and attention (with the exception of random pics taken in the moment). I hire a freelancer to choose and edit my blog post pictures, and it looks like I'll be hiring another freelancer for the motivational quote pictures as well.

Leveraging S4S To Grow Your Instagram Audience

In the slang world, S4S has two relevant meanings for this book: Share For Share and Shout Out For Shout Out. Regardless of whether you prefer shares and shout outs, the idea is to create an exchange in which you and other brands help each other grow. S4S is the epitome of the phrase "a rising wave lifts all ships" as you and someone else help each other grow your respective audiences.

Leveraging S4S begins by looking for similar Instagrammers who share other people's posts and mention others. Similar Instagrammers are in your niche and have an audience size close to yours. If you have 3,000 followers, you should ask people with 2,000 to 5,000 followers if they are interested in utilizing S4S.

It's ideal to communicate with these people through email or Instagram's direct message feature. Depending on your niche, S4S candidates may include a link to their blog within their bio. Most blogs have a Contact Me page where you can contact an Instagrammer via email. Explain that you'll promote their content in exchange for more exposure for your content.

Some people will say no, but with every yes, your audience will grow. When you get someone to agree to a S4S promotion, you just have to provide the Instagrammer with a picture for them to promote and wait for them to do the same. Some S4S promotions will be one-time partnerships while you can build other S4S partnerships to continue for months and even years later.

Don't Know What To Do?

Instagram, like any other social network, is like mastering a romance language. It first seems difficult, but as you progress, it becomes significantly easier to achieve significant results. Soon, your knowledge from Instagram can be applied to other social networks.

If you want guidelines on what you can do right now, here are four starting points.

#1: Post Daily

Each time you post a new picture on Instagram, your audience sees your content. As you begin posting pictures more often, the people within your audience start to remember you. Some people in your audience will remember you so well that they will go to your profile for new posts. In other words, they won't wait for your posts to show up in their home feed. They want to see your latest Instagram posts the moment you cross their minds.

When you post every day, you become a familiar face to the people within your audience. As more people engage with your Instagram posts, there will be certain people who you also become familiar with. This is how relationships on social media are built.

The relationships you build on social media can lead to great opportunities. Some of the relationships I built on social media led to podcast interviews, guest blogging opportunities, and more.

Finally, by posting daily, you have a stronger incentive to grow on Instagram. If you have thousands of pictures on Instagram, that is an incentive to make all of the work you put into your Instagram account worthwhile. That same incentive is not as powerful for a Twitter account (or any social network) with only five tweets. Posting daily lets you embrace Instagram, see its potential, and grow an audience of people who appreciate your content.

#2: Use Canva To Create Pictures

One of the main reasons people don't post on Instagram every day is because they don't believe they have that many pictures worth sharing. There are only so many pictures within the camera roll. What do you do when you run out of awesome pictures to share? There are two solutions:

- Take another picture
- Create a picture

I prefer creating my pictures and then posting them to Instagram. Canva is the best free tool on the web for creating pictures. You get numerous templates, background colors, and add-ons to choose from.

If you don't like their add-ons, you can always upload your own pictures (or pictures from the web) to Canva's dashboard.

#3: Consider Outsourcing The Work

The largest barrier that held me back from utilizing Instagram was time. I saw Instagram's potential but would never have the time for it. With the mix of growing my Twitter audience and now focusing most of my time on Udemy, my time was spread too thin for Instagram.

Now most of my work is outsourced. All I do on Twitter now is engage with my followers because everything else has been outsourced. All of that time I once spent following people and scheduling tweets gets devoted to other parts of my business.

Now I am putting more time and effort towards Instagram. But even now, outsourcing still reigns. I hire people to create the pictures for my Instagram account and this blog.

Outsourcing some of your Instagram activity allows you to buy back valuable time that you can repurpose into other parts of your business. Even if you don't outsource your Instagram activity, you need to outsource something in your business immediately.

#4: Use HootSuite To Schedule Posts From Your Desktop For Free

The second largest barrier holding me back from utilizing Instagram was poor desktop compatibility. Since I do most of my work on my Mac Book Pro, and Instagram isn't as optimized for the desktop as it is for mobile, I didn't spend much time on Instagram.

Then HootSuite came through in the clutch (again) by making Instagram a part of the dashboard. Now it is possible to schedule Instagram posts for free straight from the HootSuite dashboard regardless of whether you are using a mobile device or a desktop.

The bridge has finally been connected and made free for everyone. But if you do not cross that bridge to Instagram Domination, then the bridge serves no purpose. If you don't have time to schedule your Instagram posts, you can easily outsource that work to someone else so you can focus on your Instagram account's growth.

Chapter 19:

MASTERING LINKEDIN

Linkedin is the most underrated social network on the web. I like to think of the social network as Whoville. Once you hear the little whisper from the speck on the clover, you will suddenly see LinkedIn's potential and never turn back. If you don't hear the little whisper, then you don't understand why some people only create tutorials revolving around LinkedIn.

LinkedIn is more than just an online portfolio displaying your experience. Some businesses use LinkedIn to acquire more customers. Others use LinkedIn to appear on big media outlets such as *Forbes*. If your business is not on LinkedIn now, you need to start utilizing this underrated social network.

Getting more LinkedIn connections is a big factor towards success. While it's easy to reach 500+ connections and call it a day, you can connect with more people and open more doors. Here are 10 easy ways you can connect with more people on LinkedIn and effectively build your network in the process.

#1: Send Invites To The Right People

There are three things to remember about connecting with people on LinkedIn:

- Not everyone will connect with you
- Not everyone is worth connecting with
- The right connections are well worth the time it took for you to get them

Sending invites allows you to get connected with people on LinkedIn. However, you don't want to send invites to random people. You want to send these invites to highly targeted people. When I connect with people on LinkedIn, I look for social media experts, reporters, and public speakers. I look for the people I can provide value to, benefit from, and engage with.

#2: Write Meaningful Invites

Tell me if this sounds familiar:

"I'd like to add you to my professional network on LinkedIn."

It's the generic message that LinkedIn gives you for sending an invitation. Although this generic message can be edited, most people prefer to send the invitation without making any changes.

Make changes. A generic invitation is never meaningful. A meaningful invitation indicates that you actually know something about the person you are trying to connect with.

For most LinkedIn invitations I send, I spend about a minute on the person's profile and use some info from the LinkedIn profile to craft a meaningful invitation. If I want to connect with someone and have that person remember me, I dig deeper. Sometimes I'll look at someone's profile and content for 5-10 minutes just to craft the ideal invitation.

#3: Publish Posts On LinkedIn Every Day

One of LinkedIn's features is that you can publish posts on LinkedIn in the same way you would publish a blog post. You add a background picture, type the content, tag it based on LinkedIn's suggestions, and then you're all set.

Publishing posts on LinkedIn every day allows you to provide value to your connections. Some people in your LinkedIn audience may decide to share your LinkedIn posts—and by sharing, I mean doing something as simple as clicking "like" or leaving a comment (articles that your connections liked and commented on show up in your feed).

Now, you may be thinking to yourself, "How am I going to publish a new post on LinkedIn every day when I have so many other things to do?" The answer is to copy and paste your old content and make that your LinkedIn post.

This is the most time effective way to create a new LinkedIn post. Most of my LinkedIn posts are just my older blog posts. One of my first LinkedIn posts was called 100 Amazing Blogging Tips. It's based on one of my older pieces of content that needed a revival.

Publishing your older content as new LinkedIn posts doesn't hurt SEO. As long as the content gets published on your blog, channel, or podcast first, Google will understand and rank the original source higher than the

LinkedIn post. Implementing this strategy also allows you to breath new life into your old content.

#4: Engage With Other People's LinkedIn Posts

As you begin publishing your own LinkedIn posts, look within your network and begin engaging with your connections' posts. Leave a meaningful comment and like their posts.

If you like the same person's content enough times, and that person notices, that person may feel obligated to look at some of your LinkedIn posts and like them.

Repeat the process with hundreds of people on LinkedIn, and we can be talking about hundreds of likes and a few within 24 hours of you publishing your next LinkedIn post. That momentum will help your LinkedIn post get traffic within LinkedIn.

Getting more traffic within LinkedIn opens the door to more potential connections. You can also like the posts written by people you aren't connected with yet. That way, those people are likely to connect with you when you send the invitation.

#5: Leverage Your Audience

Everyone has an audience that can be leveraged. Whether you get 50 daily visitors, a blog with 1,000 daily visitors, or a few visitors here and there, you have an audience. Let your audience—that includes family and friends—know about your LinkedIn account.

The people in your audience are very likely to connect with you on LinkedIn. They already know who you are and appreciate what you do. Getting the people in your audience to connect with you on LinkedIn will give your profile a better ranking in LinkedIn's search engine.

#6: Ask For Endorsements

It is okay to ask for endorsements, but only ask the right people. Friends, family, colleagues, and people you know well on the web are the people who you can ask. Getting enough people to endorse you for certain skills will make your profile look more appealing.

An appealing profile entices people to send you invitations. While sending invitations and getting connected with people is a great strategy, it wouldn't hurt if people sent you the invitations.

When you ask for the endorsements, make sure you have them set up on your profile. Moreover, choose the best endorsements that fit what you are doing and the skill selection LinkedIn lets you choose from.

#7: Have A Professional Bio

A professional bio should mention your past professional achievements and connect them with what you do now. Strongly emphasize what you provide so people visiting your profile know if you are the right person for them to connect with.

You only want the right people to be connecting with you. If the people connecting with you have no interest in what you do, then what's the point? A professional bio lets people know who you are.

#8: Personalize Your Bio

Although staying professional is important, many people forget about the personal side. Whether they admit it or not, people are interested in what you do when you are unplugged.

What do you do when you are off of LinkedIn? What are some skills or hobbies you have that don't relate to your profession?

Adding some personalization to your bio and focusing on the professional aspect creates the perfect blend. The key reason personalization is so important is because people realize you are a human being. Now, they can relate to you.

One thing I mention is that I am a runner. I can't tell you how many conversations I have had on my social networks about running. I have talked about my fastest times and listened to other people talk about their running stories. In a sense, this interaction is fun for runners…hearing cool stories and telling our coolest stories in vivid detail.

I would have lost out on this interactions if I didn't mention I was a runner. Being a runner has nothing to do with my profession, but it sparks conversations and allows me to build deeper relationships with the people in my audience.

#9: Get Recommendations

Recommendations on LinkedIn are the most powerful type of social proof you can get from LinkedIn. In one word, LinkedIn Recommendations are testimonials.

The special thing about a recommendation is that when someone leaves a recommendation, that person's profile is linked to the recommendation. People who view your profile can see who left the recommendation, look at that person's bio, and engage with that person.

If someone on LinkedIn recommends your consultation services, savvy visitors now have the ability to directly contact your past customer. Since the customer gave you a good recommendation, that customer is bound to say good things to your potential customer.

Word of mouth doesn't sound as cool as live video, but it is as powerful as it has ever been.

#10: Utilize The Right LinkedIn Groups

LinkedIn Groups are sprouting in popularity. With their popularity, LinkedIn Groups have also generated success stories. One of the people I interviewed for my book *Lead The Stampede* tapped into a LinkedIn Group which got her featured on Forbes and amplified her message.

The right LinkedIn Groups are large and related to your niche. If a LinkedIn group has 30,000 members, there is a likelihood of a large audience reading and appreciating your content. There is also a chance that one of those people writes for Forbes.

Driving Sales & Traffic With LinkedIn

As you continue to build your Linkedin network, you'll want to cash in on your efforts. For some business owners, that means landing clients for their services. For others, it means getting your connections on your email list and getting them to buy one of your products.

The key to utilizing LinkedIn is to build relationships with your connections based on the tactics we discussed in Chapter 7. LinkedIn conversations show up in your inbox and on LinkedIn Messages which provides you with more points of contact for each of your connections.

It's also important to be clear on what you offer. This is fundamental, but even if you believe you're clear on what you offer, take a deeper look. If you offer many products and services, consider focusing most of your time, attention, and energy on a single offer. It's better to have one ultra successful product or service than it is to have 10 mediocre products or services. You can build up and offer more products and services later on, but get clear on your flagship product or service. We'll talk about creating products in the Content Monetization portion of the book, which is coming up right now.

PART 4:

CONTENT MONETIZATION

At this stage of the game, you know how to create epic content and attract people towards your content. However, if you can't capitalize on the exposure and generate revenue, you have an expensive hobby instead of a successful content brand.

We'll now discuss how to optimize your content so you can generate revenue and support yourself by creating content about the topics you love.

In this portion of *Content Marketing Secrets*, you'll come across tactics that are more than enough for generating a full-time income. For instance, some affiliate marketers make a full-time income just by promoting other people's products. Some people create training courses and make seven figures by planning out and coordinating successful launches for those training courses. Some affiliate marketers also create their own training courses. So what does this mean for you?

When you first read this book (yes, I believe you should read this book again a few months later. You'll have a new perspective and different goals, so you'll learn new things and different ideas will take shape in your mind), you'll come across the top tactics. However, the best revenue generation tactic is the one that you implement. You should start by focusing on a few revenue generation tactics rather than trying to be mediocre at all of them.

Trying to master all of the forms of revenue generation is like trying to master all of the social networks at the same time. It won't work, but it's possible after you master one of these tactics. After reading this part of the book, choose three tactics that you'll start working on.

Chapter 20:

WRITE YOUR OWN BOOK

Writing a book isn't nearly as difficult as it sounds. In fact, books may be one of the easiest info products that you can possibly create. Granted, the book has to be valuable to your targeted audience, but it's not that difficult to write a book.

I never lived in a world where you required a publisher's approval to get the ball rolling, but I've heard how difficult that world was. Now you can easily self-publish your own book without any monetary investment on your part (unless you hire someone to create your cover, edit your book, or do anything else, but the actual act of self-publishing is free).

For most of the monetization tactics I share, it's very important to have an email list to drive sales. Social media helps a little, but your email list is the asset that fills up your wallet.

The beginning step for writing your book is to come up with an idea. This idea should be similar to the type of content you're already creating. For instance, I chose to write *Content Marketing Secrets* because I create a lot of content that revolves around content marketing. More importantly, I enjoy content marketing, so make sure you create content around topics you're passionate about.

Once you have the book idea, the next step is to think of all of the possible ideas you could write about. The content marketing landscape is vast, so to prep for this book, I did a mind map of all of the different ideas I could tackle in this book.

A mind map is a piece of paper where your book title (not final at the time of the mind map) is at the center and you have a bunch of ideas surrounding the book title. These ideas will form the sections of your book. Take as much time as possible to mind map your book.

Finally, when you finished the mind mapping process, it's time to create an outline. This is where you begin to group ideas together based on how they match up with each other. Once you've completed the outline, it's time to start writing.

Writing Without Distraction

You don't need to be a great writer to write a great book. You just need the right topic, an editing process (self-editing, hiring an editor, asking people to help out, or a combination of the three), and the ideal environment filled with no distractions. Since we've already addressed the book topic and will address the editing process later, we'll tackle distractions, one of the ultimate enemies against your success.

Distractions come in many forms. Some distractions are obvious. If you've ever surfed Facebook even when you know you have an important goal, you're watching life happen instead of happening to life. If you want to eliminate those types of distractions, you can do the following:

1. Put a sticky note on your computer reaffirming your priority and that you won't get distracted on the web.

2. Eliminate the problem entirely with an app or by turning off your Wi-Fi.

3. Work in an office away from people you care about.

The first two are easier to resonate with. Putting the sticky note on your computer reinforces a positive loop where you commit to your priority and avoid distractions. My sticky notes say, "I will work on X and avoid doing Y because [why doing X is important]."

To prevent any form of temptation, I turn off the Wi-Fi when writing my book. I don't want any email notification or the thought of going on social media to take a "five minute" break. Those breaks are never five minutes long (if you use the Pomodoro technique which is repetitions of 25 minutes of working and 5 minutes of taking a break, I prefer to either stretch or stare at something other than my computer screen during those five minutes).

But the third tactic is different from the other two. The third tactic applies to people who work from home. People who work from home get to control their hours, but if you continue getting into conversations with the people you care about as you work on a big project, that big project will make little progress.

With that said, I love my family. I bend my schedule when necessary, but I'm always in isolation for at least two hours each day doing my work. By intensely working on your book, course, or any type of big project without any outside forces in the way, you will make more progress.

More importantly, you can properly switch off the business side to be fully present when with your family. If you work and continue interacting with family and friends as you work, you risk never being in the moment with those same people. I will never be the father (as of this publication, I am a long way from that stage of life, but this statement is true for me nevertheless) at my kid's sport event (or any other type of event) who is so preoccupied about work that he can't enjoy the gift of what's in front of him.

That's why I insist on working in an environment away from the people I care about. This part seems like common sense for employees and individuals who prefer to work in an office and then come home leaving the work behind. However, I understand that one of the lures to working at home is always being with your family.

Don't let work time and family time blend because you'll think about work when you're with your family, and you'll think about your family when you're working. Set boundaries that you know you can keep. This is why I wake up at 5:30 am every day. No one else is awake, and since I lose my productivity later in the day, I do family and friend related activities during that time. I don't think about my work during those times because I already did the work I had to do for the day.

However, there's another type of distraction, and this distraction doesn't feel like a distraction. If you want to find a statistic or quickly look something up that helps with your book (i.e. who coined the term "content shock?"), resist the temptation to Google your way to the answer.

If you Google your way to the answer, you'll discover Mark Schaefer coined the term in a powerful article. You'll read that article, but then you'll read more articles about content shock. Feeling tired from all of that reading, you'll go on Facebook or somewhere else.

Guess what you forgot to do? Write the book during that time.

If I ever need a statistic or verification, I put TKTK next to the part of the book I need to look over. For instance, if I didn't know who coined "Content Shock", the entry would look like this…

[A lot of text above]

"Content Shock," a term coined by TKTK, completely transformed content marketing. It made content marketers more aware of the gap between an increasing quantity of content and the fact that we still have 24 hours in a given day. Content creators realized that their content needed to stand out more than ever to attract and keep eyeballs.

[A lot of text below]

I got the TKTK idea from Tim Ferriss who uses TK when he needs to refer back to a portion of his book while editing. Few words have TK (words like Atkins), but I prefer the TKTK route because no word I know of includes TKTK without any letters in between.

I then use the word finder to locate all of the times I used TKTK in my draft. This allows me to go back and add the statistics and facts later on. With the TKTK method, my writing flow never gets disturbed because I want to verify something or find a statistic that supports a concept.

How To Speed Up The Writing Process

When some people think of writing their first book, they think of this long process that can take many months and years. However, writing your very own book doesn't have to take that long. Some authors complete their books within a few weeks while other authors even complete their books within a few days.

Here are some ways to speed up the writing process:

#1: Write On Your Smartphone

Naturally, I prefer to write a book on my computer. However, there are many situations when you can't write content on your computer…but you can do so on your smartphone.

You can use the opportune moments to develop additional chapters on your smartphone that you can then copy and paste into your book draft later. While I haven't written content for my books yet using a smartphone, I have written several blog posts that were each several thousand words long.

I view smartphone written content as free content since I would have never had that content unless I discovered this content creation hack.

#2: Video Transcription

Some people are better talkers than writers, but all of us are faster talkers than writers. While professional writers strive towards writing 100 words every minute, the casual speaker can easily surpass this milestone.

Some authors use an app like Dragon Dictation, build-in options within their smartphone, or another option to turn their speech into text during car rides. Yes, you can literally speak out your book during your daily commute.

The transcription method saves hours of time, but the editing process may take longer since you're creating your book's contents faster and more on the fly (with writing, you have slightly more time to pause and think).

#3: Hire A Ghostwriter

Sometimes the fastest way to get your book written is by not writing it at all! You can have one writer, or a team of ghostwriters, write your content for you. I still haven't hired ghostwriters for content creation, but I learned a lot about how it works after hosting the Content Marketing Success Summit. Basically, you give a ghostwriter an outline of your book's topic and he or she will write it up.

Keep in mind it's important that the ghostwriter(s) you choose are familiar with your book's topic and writing style so they can write in a similar voice. This ensures your content is consistent with your content brand (without having to write it yourself). Why not focus more of your time on other areas of your business if writing books isn't your thing?

#4: Memorize The Keyboard

Do you know where the "q" key is on your keyboard. Do you have to look down to find it? Looking down at the keyboard takes time. Although it may only take a second to look down and look up, that action makes you type slower and temporarily removes your focus from writing your book. The seconds you spend looking down at the keyboard as you write each sentence quickly add up to minutes and hours, especially if you write books and blog posts

To make up that time, you must memorize the keyboard. Your WPM (words per minute) will skyrocket and you will be less susceptible to distraction. Any moment that your fingers aren't moving quickly on the keyboard, you are susceptible to distraction.

To memorize the entire keyboard, start by memorizing all of the key placements for a single 4-5 letter word. If you can type the word "blog" with your eyes closed, you have memorized the locations of 4 of the 26 letters on the keyboard.

If you then memorize the word "each," you have memorized 8 of the 26 letters on the keyboard. Now typing a word like "beach" comes second nature as you've memorized the placements of those letters. This is a simple exercise that will allow you to write faster. This one method has saved me countless hours of time.

#5: Repurposing Your Past Content

If you have a library of content readily available, you can repurpose that content into a book. The tactics you just read on speeding up the writing process were covered in an earlier blog post.

I use the same examples and most of the wording remains intact from the original blog post. Chances are you wouldn't have known that without me telling you. In our world of information overload, it's easy to forget about blog posts we've read just a few hours ago.

Assuming they make sense for the chapter, including your past blog posts in the book is a service for your audience. Repurposing your blog posts in this manner allows you to either reinforce concepts or introduce new ideas depending on whether the reader has seen the blog post before.

You can also apply this tactic to videos and interviews. The interesting thing about this approach is that you can promote the video or interview, and some of your readers will be enticed to check it out.

Here's an example:

During my interview with Jeff Goins on Episode 50 of the Breakthrough Success Podcast, he revealed a powerful mindset for writing books. He taught Breakthrough Success listeners that "Books don't get written. Words get written. Sentences get written. Paragraphs get written…it starts small." Don't think about writing a book as writing a book. Think of the process as attaching strings of sentences and paragraphs together.

With that quick quote and reference to the Jeff Goins episode, are you slightly more interested in subscribing to the Breakthrough Success Podcast? I'm sure you won't rush to subscribe now since you're still reading, but I have succeeded at placing the podcast in your mind.

You'll come across the podcast more often through my other content, including this book. These strategic mentions add more value to my book while planting the seeds of what can result in more subscribers for my podcast at the same time.

You can create a similar effect for your videos with the following rubric:

"In my video [name of video] I shared [relevant point based on the current topic]."

You may need to slightly modify that sentence depending on the situation, but that sentence allows you to segue into the video's content while promoting your channel.

Marketing The Book For Massive Success

Without effective marketing, your book will become the greatest secret, and you won't make much revenue from your efforts. When you publish your book, you need to promote it on your email list and your social networks.

These promotional streams are common picks, and you need to promote your book on them as often as possible. In your future emails to your audience, include a 2-3 sentence postscript containing a call-to-action for your book. Tweet the book as often as possible during the week it comes out. Share it with your friends and get them to leave reviews.

However, if you start marketing your book on the day it comes out, you are missing out on a lot of opportunity. One of the best ways to promote a book is to build a book promotion team. This team of people can help with driving exposure to your book and leaving reviews on Amazon which are critical for Amazon SEO.

You can also build relationships with people in your niche and see if some of these people will promote your book to their email lists on the day it comes out. Don't turn down help as you'll need that help to get your book in front of more people.

Start your marketing at least one month before. Tell your audience that you're building a launch team, and get your launch team members involved with the book promotion. That team alone will greatly contribute to your success as an author.

Chapter 21:

TRAINING COURSES

While books are the best product for giving you instant authority in your niche, training courses are the most lucrative. In a training course, you offer your students an array of videos, PDFs, and activities that all flow towards some of the end-goals you have for each student going through the course.

Training courses are also the most profitable venture. While making 6-7 figures from a single book is extremely rare, this same accomplishment is more common with training courses. The logic behind this phenomenon is the math game associated with books and training courses.

Let's say you write a Kindle book that you price at $2.99 to capture as many sales and royalties as possible. You'll bring in about $2 from each sale. To make $100,000 from that one book, you need to sell 50,000 copies.

On the other hand, my Content Marketing Plaza training currently goes for $997. To make $100,000 in revenue, I only need to sell 101 training courses to achieve the same milestone.

Books and training courses go hand-in-hand because you can use the book to promote your training course and get even more lucrative public speaking opportunities later. However, the training course alone is the quickest and least time consuming option for reaching most of your income goals.

What To Offer In Your Training Course

Before you think about what lessons you'll cover, you need to envision the end-results of your training course. How is your student different after completing your training course? For the Content Marketing Plaza, I envisioned some of these end-results for my students:

- Learning the tactics to create content at a much faster pace so they can increase overall output
- Diversifying their content creation efforts towards blogging, video, and podcasting without an enormous amount of additional time
- Building relationships with the top players in their respective niches
- Discovering how to dominate social media and SEO so they could get thousands of monthly visitors
- Growing a targeted audience of admiring fans
- Monetizing their knowledge
- Doing all of this without working 80 hours every week

Once I envisioned some of the end-results for my students, it was easier for me to determine which videos, PDFs, and activities I needed to offer within the course. If a lesson couldn't fit with any of these envisioned end-results, I scrapped it.

You need to put that much care into your training courses because people invest their money and time to learn from you. The more time and money you ask your audience to invest in you, the more time you need to invest into making your training course the ultimate go-to place for their needs.

Create Training Courses At Different Price Points

So far, I've only talked about my $997 Content Marketing Plaza. If you have no idea who I am, then you're not investing $997 for one of my training courses. However, you would invest $7 in a tripwire training course that, through effective relationship building, would eventually result in you purchasing the Content Marketing Plaza.

It's much easier for someone to invest $7 than $997 into a training course. That's why I offer many inexpensive training course for each high-end training course I create. However, a $7 training course isn't enough. Some of the people who finish the $7 mini course will want to take an expanded training course.

They're willing to invest more of their money into your training, but asking your students to make the jump from $7 to $997 is absurd. To maximize your sales, you need to create a ladder. In my sales funnel, I like to throw in a $7, $47, $97, and sometimes a $297 courses before I tell them about the $997 course. You want to get your audience ready for the big investment.

If you don't want to go through the hassle of creating all of those additional training courses, you can provide an intense amount of free value relevant to the training course and then offer the high-end training course after providing all of that value. If you use this approach, it's best to conduct a webinar for your high-end training course ($497 and above) which we'll talk about soon.

Creating The Training Course

The only way to tap into this lucrative opportunity is to create your own training course. Creating the training course itself isn't a hard process, but you need to get clear on how you'll create it.

Basically, it comes down to one question: Are you okay with being seen on camera?

If you don't want to conduct your videos on camera yet, you can create KeyNote or PowerPoint presentations and record your computer's screen with the presentation in full display as you speak. ScreenFlow for Apple users and Camtasia for everyone else are two great tools that make screen capture and recording a breeze.

If you are happy to be seen in your videos, you have several options. You can utilize your current devices such as your smartphone, tablet, or computer. I recommend using the device that you will also use for uploading videos to your training course portal.

For instance, I use my computer to upload training videos to Vimeo. This is why I prefer to use my computer when recording videos. You don't have to transfer videos from one device to the other.

You can also use an advanced camera, but I believe those are unnecessary. Plus, most advanced cameras require that you continue buying chips, and then you need to put that chip into your computer before you can move the videos to Vimeo.

How To Publish A Training Course

Just before we discuss getting into the flow and creating the videos, you need to determine how you will publish your training course. There are two main options for publishing a training course:

#1: Places like Udemy and SkillShare: These two platforms are more beginner friendly. You just upload videos into a pre-created portal. Udemy and SkillShare will also promote your training course to their audiences. The only caveat is that Udemy and SkillShare take a percentage of your earnings for each sale depending on the type of sale you make.

#2: Unique Site: For my Content Marketing Plaza course, I preferred to host it on my own site. Hosting your own training course gives you more control over pricing and full ownership of each sale. It also means you need to create the portal yourself and set up the payment processes. This approach isn't as beginner friendly, but if this is your ideal approach, Optimize Press (member portal, video uploads, and a lot more) and SamCart (sales pages, payment processing, affiliate program, and a lot more but not as much as Optimize Press) are two tools that will help out big time. If you have your own audience and are willing to promote the course, this is the more profitable approach

Now that you know how to publish your videos in the training course format, let's talk about completing those videos.

Getting Into The Flow

The key to completing a training course is to constantly stay in the flow when producing your videos. When you shoot videos for a training course, give yourself as much time as necessary.

Every week, look for a 2-3 hour time block you can use to do nothing but create videos for your training course. A few days before that time block takes place, list all of the video topics you'd like to cover and a brief outline of what you want to cover.

For instance, if I want to do a video on 3 Ways To Monetize Your Content Brand, my outline would look like this:

3 Ways To Monetize Your Content Brand:
Training courses
Books
Affiliate marketing

Of course, we'll talk about more than three ways to monetize your content brand in this book, but that's what your outlines should look like. Each outline for each video idea should take less than a minute. You fill in the gap on game day when you're recording your videos.

For some people, I understand it's difficult for you to find 2-3 hours of uninterrupted time. While I challenge you to find those hours by waking up a little earlier or getting to bed a little later (I prefer waking up earlier), you can also do at least one video every day. That way, you do at least 30 videos every month which is more than enough videos for the typical training course.

Regardless of which working style works best for you, set a monthly goal for how many videos you'll complete. I set a goal to do 100 videos every month. On some days, I only do one video. On other days, I've done as many as 20 videos. I do most of my videos during the weekends.

Optimizing Your Training Course For Success

When you have all of your lessons laid out in your training course's portal, it's time to polish your training course for success. That means crafting an epic sales page. No matter how great the training course is, the sales page will make or break your training course.

Here are 10 staples for a great sales page:

1. **Start with a rhetorical question**. Rhetorical questions are ones that we can automatically answer without much thought. These questions allow a conversation to develop. I'll use one right now. Are you ready to dominate the content marketing landscape like never before? I already know the answer to your question, and just the mental "Yes" that ran though your head is the start of a conversation.

2. **Make it easy for people to read your description**. Use bold font, bullet points, pictures, and spacing in between paragraphs to make your sales copy feel less intimidating for your potential customers to go through.

3. **Help potential students visualize success**. If you teach people how to lose weight, describe the skinny, strong, fit body that your potential customers want. For the Content Marketing Plaza, I have people visualize the millionaire content creator.

4. **Speak to your ideal customer**. When I write about content marketing, I think about a specific customer avatar instead of my entire audience. By writing to the avatar, I effectively write for my audience. I write for someone who has no problem with putting in the work. Consistency can sometimes be an issue, but the main prob-

lem resides in marketing the content that you create. That fits the description of many people in my audience.

5. **Place the visualized success in reach**. If you have potential customers visualize success without them believing they can get there, your training courses won't have many students. You can create this effect by talking about your personal experiences of reaching this goal and/or include case studies of people who reached the goal. When introducing these stories, mention how these people started and some of their struggles so the people and stories are easier for your potential customers to connect with.

6. **Focus on benefits, not features**. People care less about what your training course offers and more about what they'll get from completing your training course. If your training course features offering 500+ videos and 6 hours of content, briefly mention it. However, it's far more important that you share benefits people will get from the course (i.e. lose 5 pounds in your first week, double your revenue in six months, etc.).

7. **Social proof**. You can utilize your own success and people's testimonials of your expertise. I recommend having at least three testimonials for your sales page although it's better to use more than three. I use social proof to demonstrate some of the places I've written for and been featured on.

8. **Several bonuses**. Offer so many bonuses that the value of your bonuses is 10 times the training course's retail price. For a $100 training courses, offer $1,000 in bonuses. Bonuses work very well, especially if they are related to your training course.

9. **Offer a money back guarantee**. We don't like getting messed over. It's happened to us all at a certain point, and with 30-day money

back guarantees as the norm, your potential customers will expect you to offer a money back guarantee as well. Some people offer 60 day money back guarantees for their training courses, but 30 days is sufficient. You don't want to offer a 7-14 day money back guarantee because your customers will think too much about the guarantee, not truly appreciate the training course experience, and be more likely to ask for their money back.

10. **Put the order button in at least three locations**. If you create your own sales page without the help of Udemy, SkillShare, or a similar place where you can publish training courses, you need to sprinkle order buttons throughout your sales page. Sales pages can get very long, and if a convinced potential customer must scroll all the way down to conduct the order, you are losing valuable time. You put in the hard work to get people on your landing page and persuade them. Don't let that milk spill. Make it as easy as possible for your potential customers to buy your training course.

By incorporating these 10 staples into your sales page, you'll entice more potential customers to enroll into your training course. At that point, it's your responsibility to deliver on the value that your customers expect.

Chapter 22:

FUNNELS

Effective funnels connect all of your targeted product offerings together to maximize your profit and the value that you provide to your audience. The funnel follows a flow that is entirely dependent on the decisions your subscribers make.

If a subscriber buys your product, you lead them into a sequence for a similar and more expensive product. If a subscriber doesn't buy your product, you continuously re-engage them and eventually mention that product again. You can continue this pattern for as long as possible. While it's common to have a $997 product at the end of your funnel, some marketers have as much as $50,000 products towards the end of their funnels (the $50,000 product can take the form of a 1-2 day mastermind at a specific location, but it can be different depending on your niche).

I suggest starting off by creating products up to the $997 price tag, getting those products to convert, and then consider adding more back-end products to your funnel.

How Should I Price My Products Up To The $997 Product?

It's difficult to land sales if you begin by asking for a $997 investment. New subscribers don't fully know you yet, so it's hard to make that sale.

Some people skip right to the $997 product during a product launch by providing a ton of free value upfront, but for an evergreen funnel, it's better to direct your subscribers towards the $997 product. Here's my preferred flow for getting people to that purchase based on the training course model:

$7 tripwire—a training course or guide that takes less than an hour to create but still contains great insights. This is the easiest investment for people to make, and it sets them up for making bigger investments in the future.

$47 training course—more value than the tripwire. This course should contain 1-3 hours of your content, but at least twice as much as your tripwire. Some people skip to a $47/mo option for a membership site in which you continually update the membership site with more content.

$97 training course—as this price tag is still under $100, you can get people who bought your $47 training course to get your $97 training course in a few minutes.

$297 training course—at each stage, you will get fewer subscribers to become customers. $297 and above is a really big investment for training courses, but at this stage, you got the subscriber to spend $151 on your past training courses. Some people will need the re-engagement sequence, but you'll get some people to buy the $297 training course.

$997 training course—for most people, this course will function as the profit maximizer. You can offer coaching and in-person meetings that exceed $997, but for now, focus on providing these five products within your funnel.

If your subscriber purchases all of these products, the total revenue is $1,445 for all of those products combined. Each of these products should segue into the other. For instance, you can offer a guide on how to create a ton of content for $7 but then provide a basic content marketing course for $47. You need the content marketing skill to get more people to see the content you create. The two products go hand-in-hand which will result in more sales.

Setting It Up

Your funnel set-up requires an advanced email service provider. I prefer to use ConvertKit for my funnels because of the tagging and trigger actions that ConvertKit provides. However, you can use a tool like SamCart or ClickFunnels to direct people to different stages in your funnel based on their purchasing decisions.

When you create your funnel email sequence, start off with the welcome email and the email sequence for your $7 tripwire. Write the email sequences in order from least expensive product to most expensive product. The email sequences for your least expensive products will get more visibility than your high-ticket products.

With that said, you still want epic copy for your high-ticket products because out of that $1,445 maximum value, the $997 training course constitutes 69% of that maximum value and the $297 training course constitutes 21% of that total value (90% for both of them). The other training courses and tripwire help your subscribers get more comfortable with making bigger investments in your products and services.

Here is the basic email sequence that you should follow. Any purchase leads the subscriber to the next funnel.

Funnel #1:

1. Offer a free guide/resource to get the email address. *Repeatedly mention the tripwire in this freebie because it's easy to get an upfront $7 sale*
2. Send a follow-up email a day later asking if the new subscriber read/watched your free resource and mention you have something special for them inside (the tripwire)
3. Follow-up with two emails about your tripwire each spaced out by 2 days.

Funnels #2-5:

1. Immediately thank the subscriber for purchasing the product from the previous funnel.
2. Provide 2-3 emails of free value each spaced 1-2 days apart. This type of value is strategic. It creates demand for your next product and eliminates excuses. For instance, referring back to my $7 content creation tripwire and my $47 basic content marketing course, I provide free content on how content creators can find the time to promote & create (breaking the lack of time excuse) and a few tactics for getting more results from their marketing efforts (the more valuable your free content is, the more perceived value your subscribers will assign to your products).
3. Craft two soft sell emails and a hard sell email each spaced 2-3 days apart. Send the first soft sell email two days after the last free value email. The hard sell email goes second and your final soft sell email ends off the sequence.

4. If a subscriber doesn't buy your product, put them in a re-engagement sequence which focuses on providing free value. As your subscribers engage with more of your free value emails, you can begin offering products again, even if the product is different from the product the subscriber previously turned down. Just make sure the product matches up with the free value you've been providing.

Optimizing Your Results

Once you have created each part of the funnel, you must treat each part as its own separate entity that you can develop. I'll use some basic math to demonstrate this concept (if you know how to add, subtract, multiply, and divide, you have all of the knowledge you need). Let's say you get 10,000 people in your funnel.

$7 tripwire at a 20% conversion rate—2,000 sales

$47 training course at 10% conversion rate—200

$97 training course at a 10% conversion rate—20

$297 training course at a 10% conversion rate—2

$997 training course at a 10% conversion rate—1 (rounding up from .2)

Your tripwire will by far convert better than your other offers sheerly due to price. As you advance through the funnel, you will see fewer sales but more revenue per sale. If you increase the conversion rate of any of your products, you increase sales for all of your products. For instance, let's say you have a 30% conversion rate for your tripwire and everything else remains the same.

$7 tripwire at a 30% conversion rate—3,000 sales

$47 training course at 10% conversion rate—300

$97 training course at a 10% conversion rate—30

$297 training course at a 10% conversion rate—3

$997 training course at a 10% conversion rate—1 (rounding up from .3)

A slight percentage increase in your conversion rate for any of your products can net thousands of extra dollars. Not only do you increase product sales for one of your products, but you also get more people into your funnels for your more expensive products. The only two ways you can increase sales for your funnel are to get more people into your funnel and increase the conversion rates of your landing pages and products.

Skipping To The $997 Product

While it's not recommended to skip to this product at the beginning of a relationship, you can provide massive upfront free value and then lead into this product. I only recommend leading right into the $997 product if you host a virtual summit with many speakers, but you can also promote your high-end products to the people who have been on your email list for a while.

After receiving months and years of your free content, people will be more open to investing $997 towards one of your products or services. You can promote the high-end product to your audience once every 4-6 months so the $997 product still gets sales, but you aren't annoying your audience with over promotion.

With that said, virtual summits can expedite the relationship between you and new subscribers many months and years down the road in a matter of days. You can get some of your virtual summit attendees to purchase your $997 product even if they didn't know who you were before the virtual summit. Why are virtual summits such an exception and lucrative opportunity? That's what we'll discuss in the next chapter.

Chapter 23:

VIRTUAL SUMMITS

Organizing and hosting a virtual summit is a herculean task that can pay off in a big way. The concept behind a virtual summit is gathering dozens of speakers together in one virtual place so attendees don't have to travel to see their favorite speakers in action.

You should have a minimum of 20 speakers for your virtual summit, but some summits go above 50 speakers. Each virtual summit has its different recipe for success, but I prefer to have at least 50 speakers for my virtual summits.

All of the sessions are free for 24-72 hours after they get released to the public. After that time expires, they get put into a vault that attendees can only access if they purchase an All-Access Pass. I start off with a $67 All-Access Pass and bump up the price as the days go by. I typically bump my All-Access Pass price as high as $297 and let my attendees know when I'll bump the price to create urgency.

At the end of your virtual summit, you then host a webinar to sell your $997 product within that webinar. After the webinar, you send out a few emails to get some last minute sales. For any high-ticket product, most of your sales will come at the beginning and end of the promotion.

The cool part about virtual summits is that they are amazing for audience growth. If you get the speakers and some affiliates to promote the virtual summit, you will get some people from all of their audiences to become a part of your audience. Some virtual summits attract tens of thousands of attendees which you can email during the summit and even afterwards.

How To Land Speakers For Your Summit

Before you focus on attracting attendees, you need to attract speakers for your summit. They form the experience and eventually an entirely new product (your All-Access Pass). The best way to land speakers for your virtual summit is to leverage your current connections. I was lucky enough to know legends like Ray Edwards, David Jenyns, Matt McWilliams, Aaron Orendorff, and plenty of others before the summit started. I landed close to 10 speakers with my existing connections.

When you begin your search for speakers outside your network, look for speakers who have spoken at past virtual summits that are similar to yours. For the Content Marketing Success Summit, I looked for speakers at the Authority Super Summit and the Self-Publishing Success Summit. These virtual summits showcased speakers who I knew would be a great fit for my summit. I contacted speakers one by one with this message:

> Hello [name],
> I am organizing my virtual Content Marketing Success Summit and was wondering if you'd like to be one of the speakers. We'd discuss [topic] or something else you prefer. If you are interested, I'll send an email containing more details about the event. It would be awesome to have you on board.
> [Closing]

This email is not a hard pitch at all. I provide a topic so the speaker doesn't have to decide on a topic, but I offer the opportunity to talk about another topic during the session. In addition, I will only send more info if the potential speaker is interested in learning more.

After I get that yes, I send more info, and when you send over the info, you'll almost always get a yes after that. The additional info comes as a 5-page PDF. Here's what each page contains:

Page 1: Your virtual summit's logo and dates. Speakers need to know if the scheduling matches up with their email promotion plans.

Page 2: Your virtual summit's structure. Most summits consist of 3-4 parts. The four parts for CMSS are Content Creation, Content Marketing, Social Media Marketing, and Content Monetization

Page 3: Are interviews conducted on Skype or Zoom (please use Zoom for your own sake)? Where do the videos go? When do speakers get the questions? When do you need the pre-recorded interviews done by? All of the answers to these questions need a 1-2 line bullet point. If you have a link to your online calendar showing your availability (I use Acuity to do this for $9.99/mo. One of the best investments you can make for a virtual summit for saving time), include the link on that page.

Page 4: Your request for speakers. Typically, I ask speakers to promote the summit to their audiences at least once. I also provide some email plans for speakers who want to go all-in with the promotion. I also mention that speakers receive affiliate links, so there's an added incentive to promote the virtual summit.

Page 5: Goals for the summit. For your first virtual summit, state that you want X speakers. After your first virtual summit, state a goal for how many attendees you want since you have more experience.

Each page is a series of bullet points. Most of my pages have under 50 words total. Create the PDF as if it's a PowerPoint or KeyNote presentation. As the Apple lover I am, I used KeyNote to create the PDF. You simply create all of the slides and then export the entire presentation as a PDF.

As you get more speakers, change your pitch to look like this:

> Hello [name],
>
> I am organizing my virtual Content Marketing Success Summit and was wondering if you'd like to be one of the speakers. Speaker 1, Speaker 2, and Speaker 3 are among the 50+ (**change to your number to the anticipated total, not what you have now**) speakers who will share their insights to the attendees. We'd discuss [topic] or something else you prefer. If you are interested, I'll send an email containing more details about the event. It would be awesome to have you on board.
>
> [Closing]

Mentioning specific speakers will build up social proof for your virtual summit. Some potential speakers will think, "Wow, I get to speak with those influencers. I've got to jump on this."

Scheduling The Interviews

Once you get a speaker's commitment, you can proceed to schedule the interview. You can do the back-and-forth exchanges until you find a time and date that work for you, but I strongly recommend against it. You're better off using a tool like Acuity to display your availability and let speakers choose times and dates that work for both of you. It will save you a ton of time you'd have to use sending unnecessary back-and-forth emails and staying organized.

Depending on the time you have from idea to kickoff date, here are some approaches for scheduling the interviews:

#1: If your summit kickoff is approaching soon (1-2 months), aim to get all of the interviews done within a 2-3 week window

#2: You can follow that same approach regardless of how much time you have before your summit kickoff, but if you have more than three months to prepare, you can choose 2-3 days of the week to conduct interviews so you have 4-5 days to utilize towards other activities.

How To Prepare For Each Interview

Each session has this basic workflow:

- You greet the attendees, introduce the topic, and introduce the speaker
- You ask questions
- You give the speaker the chance to promote himself/herself

The questions you ask depend on the overall topic, but I like to ask everyone the same 2-3 questions. This framework allows me to write up fewer questions but still have a 30 minute session. When writing the questions, I think of the speaker as a consultant and me as the client. What is it that I would like to know that my attendees would also like to know?

While asking great questions depends on the topic, you can utilize a rubric for all of your introduction. For instance, here's the rubric I used for the Content Marketing Success Summit:

> Hello and welcome to the Content Marketing Success Summit. It's a pleasure to have everyone here today. [1-2 sentences leading into topic and briefly showing why it's important]. We'll show you how to do just that…right now!
>
> For this session, I'm bringing in [name of speaker] to discuss [name of topic]. [3-4 sentences about speaker which you can usually find on the speaker's about me page]. With that said, it's time for less talking and more action!
>
> [Name of speaker], it's a pleasure to have you on [acronym OR name of your summit]!

That's all it takes to craft a great introduction for your virtual summit. The introduction will make or break the quality of your interview, so handle it with care and be very enthusiastic as you read it off your computer screen.

After the introduction, you'll proceed to ask the questions as you wrote them. During this portion of the interview, you want to listen while remaining the host. As you listen to the speaker's answer, think of how you'll quickly sum up that answer and pivot towards the next question.

Let's say I ask two questions in this order:

1. How do you grow your email list?
2. How do you keep that email list engaged?

While this is more on the fly, I might use this segue between those questions:

[Name of speaker], thank you for sharing those insights on how to grow an email list. However, if we grow an email list but don't get any engagement, then we have wasted a very valuable asset. So, how can we keep our email lists engaged with our content?

Some pivots are easier to make than others. You have to think of how you'll make the pivot as the host but also listen to what the other person is saying. You're an attendee too, and you can learn a lot about your niche by organizing a virtual summit! To this day, I re-watch some of the CMSS interviews to gather more insights and come across old ideas with a new frame of mind.

Maximizing Your Virtual Summit's Revenue

I could write an entire book on hosting and organizing your virtual summit, but I'll conclude by sharing how you can maximize your virtual summit's revenue. Getting partners with large audiences to promote your virtual summit is a big plus, but what about the entire experience? How can you monetize the virtual summit experience as effectively as possible?

For maximum revenue, the sales start immediately upon subscription. When a visitor enters their name and email address to become an attendee, they get redirected to what I like to call a "Thank You Sales Page." I thank the visitor for becoming an attendee and tell them that their info will come shortly.

However, I also state that I want to tell the new attendee about the All-Access Pass. On this Thank You Sales Page is a video about the All-Access Pass and all of the benefits you get from purchasing it.

For my $47 All-Access Pass (the price has increased since then), I provided $585 of additional value in the form of extra training. The icing on the cake is a 15 minute timer that, once expired, leads people to a more expensive All-Access Pass. That means new attendees only have 15 minutes to decide whether to buy the All-Access Pass at its discounted price or not, and this sense of urgency drives a lot of sales.

For my All-Access Pass order page, I give customers the option to add my Blog Post Promotion Blueprint to their order. It's less expensive than the All-Access Pass, and it only takes one click to add the blueprint to their final order (you can get this capability with SamCart and ClickFunnels). Adding this one training course as an order bump increased my summit revenue by about 20%.

After someone purchases your All-Access Pass, you can even lead your new customers to another Thank You Sales Page for a similar product and continue the pattern for as long as you desire. Leverage one-click order bumps as often as possible.

Chapter 24:

AFFILIATE MARKETING

Affiliate marketing is arguably the most important form of marketing to master. Not only can you receive commissions by promoting other people's products, but you tap into the affiliate marketer's mindset—an important mindset for building relationships and organizing joint ventures.

We'll start this chapter off with affiliate marketing from the affiliate's point of view and then capitalizing on this trend by creating your own joint ventures.

Finding The Right Offers

There are countless products that you can promote as an affiliate marketer. Training courses, books, toys, and even a box of tissues are all fair game. Before I focused on promoting training courses and books, I promoted LEGO sets and Yugioh Cards through Amazon's affiliate program.

Countless options is a blessing, but it is also a curse. If you choose the wrong affiliate offers to focus on, you'll leave thousands of dollars on the table. Promoting products as an Amazon affiliate meant only receiving a 4% commission on what I sold. I could bump that commission to 10% if I got a large enough quantity of sales, but even then, 10% of a commission for a $50 LEGO set is just an extra $5. Some people find success with the Amazon Associate model, but it wasn't working for me.

What works for me is promoting relevant training courses to my audience and making hundreds of dollars from every sale. Most training courses I promote go from $997 to $1997, and depending on the course, I get a 40-50% commission for each sale. One $997 training course sale at a 40% commission rate lands me $398.80. To land that same figure with LEGO sets, I would need to sell almost $10,000 worth of LEGO sets to make the same commission.

When looking around for offers, you must look for the following:

1. **An offer with a good commission for each sale**. This definition differs for each person's niche, but I promote products that can bring in at least $100 per sale AND convert very well. If I get $5,000 per sale but make no sales, then I was better off promoting something else.

2. **An offer relevant to my niche**. I don't promote LEGO sets anymore because they have nothing to do with my niche. Furthermore, I am careful with which training courses I promote. I'll promote Ray Edwards' Copywriting Academy because writing great copy is critical for boosting your sales.

3. **Proven concept**. When I promote Jeff Walker's Product Launch Formula, I'm not worried about whether this promotion will bring in sales. I know promoting PLF will result in sales because Jeff makes seven figures from all of his launches. You can only do that if you're rocking an epic conversion rate and have a lot of partners promoting your training course.

4. **Time investment**. If it takes two months of my time to promote a single offer, that's way too much. I hover towards the offers that require 2-4 weeks of my attention. Sometimes I'll send out a random email promoting something, but I typically look for affiliate offers that require emails to my list for 2-4 weeks. That's enough time to build the relationship and get sales without being overbearing or restricting my ability to jump on other affiliate offers.

5. **Webinars are not optional**. In my niche, hosting a webinar where you eventually sell your training is one of the most powerful ways to drive sales. If there's no webinar in the launch plan, I will look for another affiliate offer.

Tactics For Affiliate Marketing Success

Once you find the ideal offer to promote to your audience, it's time to plan out your promotion. This planning stage will help you get more sales, and while some affiliate programs cover the planning (i.e. here's when and how to promote this, that, and the other thing), you should formulate your own plan as well.

Here are some tactics that will help you see more success in your promotions as an affiliate marketer.

#1: Promote on the bookends of open cart. The two most important days for sales are the day the cart opens and on the day the cart closes. Some people will immediately purchase what you're offering while others need a little nudge and a sense of urgency towards the end to make their purchases. Emailing in between this gap helps some people get over the fence and buy on close cart day.

#2: Give people a reason to take action. Offering a bonus for people who buy through your affiliate link is a common tactic for boosting sales. While I recommend it, you should also offer small bonuses for all actions taken throughout the process. If you promote an affiliate offer where you get people to subscribe to get access to a free video, ask your audience to share one of their key takeaways from that video. Then, respond with your key takeaway or offer a free video of your own on a similar topic. That will increase your audience's engagement throughout the promotion.

#3: Email your unopens. One of the easiest ways to increase an email's clickthrough and open rates is to resend the same email with a different subject line to everyone who didn't open it the first time. Send enough of these emails throughout the promotion, and you could make a bunch of extra sales that you wouldn't have made otherwise.

#4: Create product reviews for evergreen offers. Product reviews give your audience a glimpse into what a product can offer for them. If you offer an honest review that tackles pros and cons, you can attract the right customers. It's important to offer the cons as well because if you don't, you'll probably get more refunds since customers weren't anticipating those cons.

#5: Create a resources page for evergreen offers. This goes along the same lines as product reviews. The only difference is that you list all of the resources you use. For instance, I use ConvertKit to send my emails, and they are a resource I include on my resources page. You can categorize your resources page based on the type of product so it's easier for your visitors to find the specific type of resource they're looking for (i.e. affiliate marketing tool versus a training course).

#6: Use affiliate links anytime you mention the product or service in a blog post. If you are an affiliate for ConvertKit, and you mention ConvertKit in a blog post, the word ConvertKit should be a link that, when clicked on, leads to your affiliate link. You can do this for any product in your niche. Only hyperlink the first reference of the product or service you use because you don't want your blog posts to be seen as spammy.

#7: Listen to your audience. I have promoted many affiliate offers, and I stick with the most successful ones. As of this book, my most successful affiliate promotions are the Copywriting Academy and Self-Publishing School, so I continue promoting those training courses and ones that are similar.

Organizing Your Own Joint Ventures

Once you promote some affiliate offers, you'll have enough experience to organize your own joint ventures. You'll need to recruit affiliates and communicate with them so everyone is on the same page.

If you have the budget, I recommend hiring an affiliate manager to recruit and communicate with affiliates. However, I understand that some people don't have that option. Although it will take more time, you can find affiliates and communicate with them on your own.

Finding Affiliates

There are plenty of ways you can find affiliates. You can start by looking back at what products you have promoted in the past. Many people post online reviews of affiliate products, and you can begin contacting people who reviewed that affiliate product and other products related to what you're offering.

Depending on the affiliate program you're in, you may have access to a leaderboard which displays the names of the top affiliates in an affiliate competition. You can contact these people one-by-one and let them know about your affiliate program.

You can also send an email to your subscribers and let them know that you're running an affiliate program. I got dozens of affiliates from my email list to help with the CMSS promotion. Once you have those people on board, you can make a power move and offer 2nd-tier commissions for all of the affiliates that they refer to your affiliate program. Now you'll have more people promoting your offer, you'll make more revenue, your affiliates who referred their friends also make more revenue, and the new affiliates get to make sales too. It's a win-win-win!

You can also find affiliates at in-person conferences and events. While I haven't done this on my own, affiliate marketing legend Matt McWilliams often uses this tactic to recruit new affiliates and strengthen relationships with his current affiliates who happen to be at the same conference or event.

Communicating With Affiliates

Once you have an army of affiliates ready to promote your offer, you must communicate with them to ensure you're all on the same page. The last thing you want in a joint venture promotion is to recruit the affiliates but hinder their potential and your earnings because of poor communication.

That's why you need multiple points of communication. For my joint venture promotions, I create a custom email list and put all of my affiliates into the partners Facebook Group page. That way, affiliates can either see the latest news through an email or my Facebook post.

Once you have these two communication platforms established, the rate of conversation depends on what stage you're in. A few days away from launch and during the actual launch, you need to communicate with your affiliates at least once per day on both platforms. If you want your affiliates to email their lists, give them swipe copy and their affiliate link within the email.

Make all of the necessary information about your launch, including the promotional plan (i.e. when to promote what), as easy for your affiliates to access as possible. It's also helpful to shoot a video a few days before the promotion starts where you share how affiliates can get more sales from their efforts.

Once you have the affiliate army and communication set up, you can rock your joint venture promotion. Joint ventures are truly the most lucrative marketing opportunity because you get an army of many people putting you in front of their audiences. Regardless of which type of product or service you create, joint ventures will exponentially increase your revenue. It helps to engage in some affiliate marketing beforehand so you can make the most out of this opportunity.

Chapter 25:

COACHING, CONSULTATIONS, & OTHER SERVICES

Offering coaching, consulting, or another service (i.e. a done for you service in your niche) presents an interesting opportunity for revenue generation. The big advantage with offering a service is that you are the product. You don't need to write thousands of words for your upcoming book or make videos and create a training course.

Upon receiving the payment, you spend your time helping your customer getting close to a specific goal. You don't need to create the product as mentioned before, but this model does offer its challenges. Everything's smooth sailing when you have 1-5 clients, but the moment you have more than 5 clients, continuing to offer your services will take up more of your time. The more clients you take in, the less time you have to explore opportunities and maintain your work-life balance.

3 Ways To Fix The Over Capacity Problem

If you want to offer a service, you need to think about fixing the over capacity problem now. In other words, if offering services if your thing, but you don't have a plan for welcoming Client #100 and giving all

100 clients the ongoing quality service that they expect, then there's a problem. Luckily, there are some ways to fix the problem.

1. **Offer a one-off service**. While coaching involves a constant investment of your time towards your client's success, offering consultations requires a one-off time commitment unless your client decides to purchase another consultation session. There's more revenue to be made with the coaching model, but if you find yourself in an overflow of clients, you may want to start with consultations or offer both.

2. **Delegate parts or even all of the process**. Have you ever tried to be coached by a super successful person. In many cases, these people have certified coaches who help them out. My friend Matt McWilliams has a coaching program where he himself coaches people, but he also has a team of coaches in place for 50% off. Matt charges $15,000 for 10 hours of his time, but you can get someone on Matt's team for $7,500 for the same timeframe. He's making it more tempting to get coached by someone on his team because it's very stressful to coach dozens of clients (and eventually hundreds), get everything else done, and spend time with the important people in your life. As social media services become more popular, the service providers tend to hire people to do the work so they can focus more of their time on growing the business. They did the initial work, and now trustworthy employees continue to carry out that work.

3. **Set a limit**. If you don't want to delegate for now and find that you can't handle more than 5 clients, then don't bring in Client #6. I know it's hard to turn down clients who will bring more revenue to your business, but it's better to have 5 clients who you treat well than 10 clients who you don't treat well. With that said, you can

drop a client to make room for a new client, but I only recommend this course of action if you really love the prospect and absolutely despise one of the clients you are helping. This approach limits your growth, but it can be solved later on with delegation.

Pricing Your Services

As mentioned before, Matt McWilliams charges $15,000 for 10 virtual hours with him. He can charge at $1,500/hr (and he charges more per hour when you purchase less time) because he's organized launches for people like Ray Edwards, Jeff Goins, Brian Tracy, Chandler Bolt, the Ziglar Family, and a lot more. Some people charge thousands of dollars every hour while other people can't get clients with a $100/hr or $300/mo service. Why can some people charge premium prices and have clients swarming to their services while other people charge relatively low prices but can't get any takers?

The main answer to that question is the perceived value of the service. A coaching call with Tony Robbins has more perceived value than a coaching call with the average motivational coach. You know Tony will share some legendary advice with you because of his work and impact on the world, but you don't know how an up-and-coming motivational coach will perform.

You can increase the perceived value of your services by producing meaningful work and getting as many testimonials as possible from clients, blog visitors, and anyone else you can think of. There's no such thing as having too many testimonials. Your authority, social proof (i.e. testimonials and audience size), and work determine the perceived value of your services. The higher your perceived value, the more you can charge, and then it's up to you to live up to the perceived value.

One final important note is that the price of your services will affect the total number of clients. With everything else equal, you won't get as many clients charging Matt McWilliams' prices as the individual with $100/hr consultation sessions. In the beginning, it's good to get a lot of clients with consultation sessions because this approach equips you with more experience and testimonials.

However, let's say you get that $15,000 sale and give your client 10 hours of your time. You know how many clients you would need for the $100/hr consultation sessions? A grand total of 150 clients…and 150 hours of your time. The high-ticket service price results in fewer clients, but in this example, the one $15,000 sale saves you time finding 149 additional clients and saves you an extra 140 hours that you would then invest towards serving those clients.

In the long-term, aim for higher price points to decrease the number of your clients but increase the revenue you make from each client. It's easier to form a meaningful one-on-one relationship with a $15,000 client than it is to form a meaningful one-on-one relationship with 150 clients giving you $100 each. You make the same revenue, but save a massive amount of time and deliver more value into the relationship.

How To Get Clients

The best way to get more clients is to consistently grow your audience using the Content Marketing and Social Media Marketing tactics within this book. Most importantly, you need to grow your email list because that's where all of the magic happens.

However, you can find clients in your current network. Your family and friends may know someone who can use your services. When you land your first quality client, do your service as effectively as possible. You should always respect the fact that your clients invested their time and money into your services, but the first quality client is particularly important. That's because quality clients tend to know other people who would be great clients for your services. The better you serve your clients, the more likely you are to get referrals.

In the beginning, many client-based businesses are built on referrals. Your business will always spread due to word-of-mouth, and if that word-of-mouth is good, referrals will always play a key role in growth.

The Money Is In The Follow-Up

With any opportunity worth pursuing, victory lies within the follow-up. Some people will express interest in your services, but then they get busy and forget about you. Other people need a small nudge before committing to your services.

If a prospect expresses interest but communication soon stops, reach out to that same prospect within a week and ask if they're still interested. You can even engage with old clients and ask them if they need additional help. Following up with your old and new connections will work wonders not just for client acquisition, but for any goal you set for yourself.

Scaling Up

If you only learn one thing from this chapter, I want you to come away with the fact that if you are serious about offering a service, you need a plan for welcoming Client #100 while continuing to provide great value for the other 99 clients. We briefly touched on delegation earlier, but we will now expand on this concept to scale up your services.

As you serve more clients, pay attention to every task you perform for your clients. What do you love to do? What do you not enjoy so much? What's a task that anyone can do with the proper training?

The tasks you outsource are dependent on the type of service you offer. Let's say that you coach your clients and offer a one-page report which summarizes the conversation. Instead of you writing that report, you can hire someone else to write that report for you. Just send a recording of your conversation, and your writer is off to the races. If it takes you an hour to write that one-page report, then you have that extra hour to acquire and serve more clients.

Now let's imagine this on a larger scale. Let's say all you had to do was build the relationship with your client and check in on their progress once every two weeks as your team handles all of the work. With this set-up, you can greet Client #100 and have 99 happy clients greeting the 100th client with you. Of course, this level of delegation is easier said than done, but it all starts with one task.

Find the one unenjoyable task that takes up a good amount of your time. You may despise writing that one-page report but know that your clients love them. When you post your job description on a place like UpWork, get clear on what the job entails. Write the job description as if the job applicants have no idea how to write one of your reports (they don't). Write down as many questions you would have as a potential employee, and answer them in your description. If you wanted me to write those one-page reports, here are some questions I would have:

1. Single spaced or double spaced? Is there a minimum word count?
2. Bullet points or long paragraphs?
3. How do I start and conclude?
4. What are the important points I need to cover in the report?
5. How will you communicate what I need to focus on in the report?

The more effort you put towards your job description, the more likely you are to get applicants who know the requirements and can do a great job. A vague job description invites more applicants which isn't necessarily a good thing because you have to find the needle in a big haystack. A clear and concise job description puts more needles in a much smaller haystack.

When you first hire someone, micromanage that person for a week. Say what you like and don't like about their work and teach them how to do the task the way you would. There will be a learning curve and a communication curve, but after a week of micromanaging, quality employees don't need as much supervision. At that point, a weekly check-in will work unless your employee asks a question or wants help with something.

Scaling up is one of the most exciting times for a content brand. More people come across your message and you generate more revenue which breathes more life and opportunity into your content brand. Start with the small step of hiring one person to perform a task that is necessary but not essential for your success. Then expand from there.

Chapter 26:

SET FORTH

When I wrote this book, I reflected on my journey. I reflected on my triumphs and missteps. Every day is a new beginning within our blogging journey. We can either accomplish so much or so little within the 24 hours that we are given each day.

With the knowledge you've obtained from this book, it's now time for you to embrace a new beginning within your journey. I hope the possibilities this book introduced with you will motivate you to pursue bigger goals. Don't be afraid to dream big. Towards the end of 2012, my big dream was surpassing 100,000 Twitter followers by the end of 2017. It was my five year plan. I grew my Twitter audience well past 100,000 followers by that five year deadline. I didn't achieve this goal by dreaming small. I achieved that goal by dreaming big and exerting massive action towards that goal.

If you dream of surpassing 100,000 monthly visitors within the next 12 months, you can! Just believe in yourself and put in the work. An activity that works wonders is telling the world about your goals. Dare yourself to dream bigger and tell more people about your dream. You'll then ignite the action-taker in you and build the content empire of your dreams.

ABOUT THE AUTHOR

Marc Guberti is a digital marketing expert and the host of the Breakthrough Success Podcast. Marc started his first blog when he was 11, and through trial-and-error, grew his content brand. Marc has also hosted and organized virtual summits like the Content Marketing Success Summit and Productivity Virtual Summit where he interviews the top influencers to discover new insights. Marc's Blog has a free library of content stuffed to the gills with insights on digital marketing, entrepreneurship, and productivity.

Marc believes that age is not a limit to success. He was still a teen when this book was written and published. He believes that by producing valuable work as a teen and continuing past his teens, he can show other teens with dreams what's possible for them. This desire to show others what is possible is why Marc ends his emails with "Dream big, achieve greatness, and unlock your potential…TODAY!!"

THANK YOU FOR READING MY BOOK!

I am very appreciative that you chose to read this book all the way through. My mission as an author is to provide content that allows people to take action and achieve better results.

If you enjoyed the book, <u>I would be grateful if you could leave a quick review</u>. Reviews will help other readers know if this is the right book for them.

Thank you!

—**Marc Guberti**

Made in the USA
Middletown, DE
11 August 2018